NORTHLAND WILD FLOWERS

A Guide for the Minnesota Region

The seventh printing of this book was made possible in part by
a grant from the Hamilton P. Traub University Press Fund.

NORTHLAND WILD FLOWERS

A Guide for the Minnesota Region

John B. Moyle
and
Evelyn W. Moyle

University of Minnesota Press, Minneapolis

Published by the University of Minnesota Press
111 Third Avenue South, Suite 290, Minneapolis, MN 55401-2520
Printed in the United States of America on acid-free paper
Seventh printing, 1997

Library of Congress Catalog Card Number 76-55173

ISBN 0-8166-0806-7
ISBN 0-8166-1355-9 (pbk.)

Dedication

To Walter John Moyle, horticulturist, and
Carl Otto Rosendahl, botanist and teacher,
both of whom knew and enjoyed the wild
flowers, and to all who are helping preserve
our wild flower heritage.

Preface

This book is for those who enjoy the Northland wild flowers and would like to know more about them. Basically it is about those kinds found in Minnesota but should also be useful in the similar northern landscapes of adjacent areas. Plants recognize no geographic boundaries. It is a book that we hope will benefit both the reader and the wild flowers. Wild flowers are an important part of our natural and cultural heritage — a heritage that provides much outdoor enjoyment and needs our understanding and help for preservation in the future.

Included are color photographs of 300 wild flowers and text material on these and about 100 other kinds. Botanical terminology has been kept to a minimum. Some of the more common wild flowers habitats are also illustrated. Places and times for seeing wild flowers are suggested and items of general botanical and cultural interest are often included.

We are grateful to many wild flower enthusiasts for suggestions, encouragement, companionship afield, and friendly advice both botanical and photographic. We wish especially to thank Mr. John McKane, Dr. John W. Moore, Dr. and Mrs. Lloyd Smith Jr., Dr. Walter Breckenridge, Mr. and Mrs. Ralph Forester, Mr. John Dobie, Mr. Rupert Lowrey, Dr. Max Partch, and Mr. William Longley. The photograph of Stiff Tickseed was supplied by Mr. Dobie, that of Calypso by Mr. John Mathisen, that of Wintergreen in fruit by Walter M. Moyle and that of Fringed Gentian by Ruth E. Moyle.

J.B.M. and E.W.M.

Table of Contents

🌼🌼🌼🌼🌼🌼🌼🌼🌼🌼🌼🌼🌼🌼🌼🌼

🌼🌼🌼🌼🌼🌼🌼🌼🌼🌼🌼🌼🌼

NORTHLAND WILD FLOWERS

A Guide for the Minnesota Region

With a hi ho
And a hey nonny nonny
And the Northland flowers
Spring so bonny

And so it is in the Northland that is Minnesota and the adjacent landscapes. Winter may be long and cold, but with spring come the wild flowers that brighten the countryside until the frosts of autumn. There are many kinds of wild flowers and they grow in many places.

Of the 1700 species of flowering plants that are wild in Minnesota, about one-quarter might be considered wild flowers. Wild flowers are easily recognized but as a group are difficult to define. Whether a wild plant is a wild flower depends upon its appearance, where it grows, and who sees it. It could be a wild flower, a weed, or just a bit of natural greenery, depending upon your point of view. Generally we have selected herbs with colorful or otherwise interesting flowers. Some have or have had practical uses, some have interesting historical connections, but most are just colorful wild flowers that were waiting there as good photographic subjects. The entire growing season is represented, but emphasis is placed on the wild flowers of late summer and autumn. These late comers deserve to be better known. Spring is a pleasant season and the time for woodland wild flowers, but in autumn the open roadsides and prairies are the most colorful.

Wild flowers are for seeing, but primarily for seeing by insects. Like many birds and like us, insects have color vision. The color of wild flowers, as well as their odor and nectar, attracts insects and encourages them to visit and pollinate flowers, often those of a particular type. Watch a bee or some other insect working on flowers. Usually it does not visit flowers at random but rather goes from flower to flower of the same kind. The varied shapes and color patterns of wild flowers, some of which, like the lady-slippers, are marvelously complex, are stratagems by which cross-pollination is made more certain. By cross-pollination the genetic inheritance of a plant is maintained, reshuffled, and renewed. Over their long history, plants and insects have developed together to their mutual benefit.

Wild flowers also should be understood for the satisfaction that comes with understanding. Flowers and fruits provide the keys to natural relationships of plants and for the most part are the characteristics by which plants can be grouped into families and genera. Understanding such relationships of the more than 250,000 flowering plants of this green world is one of the great achievements of the human mind and is a cornerstone of natural science.

In a broad developmental sense wild flowers and other wild plants are as successful as we are — they are here. In the long history of survival each has developed variations on the general life forms and processes, including the biochemical. Each produces many kinds of chemical compounds. Some have been useful to us as drugs (quinine and digitalis are examples) or for other purposes. From a practical viewpoint alone, we should take care not to lose the wild plants that can produce complex substances whose value is as yet unknown but which we may sometime need.

Plant Names

Wild flowers and other plants have two kinds of names — common and botanical. The common names for the wild flowers included here are those most generally used and accepted in this area. Usually they are the names recognized in botanical manuals, guides, and checklists. Often, however, a wild flower has several common names, and sometimes several wild flowers share the same common name. In some cases, especially for uncommon kinds of plants, the common name is an obvious translation of the botanical name.

Botanical names, which consist of two Latin or Latinized words, have the advantage of being accepted by botanists worldwide. Theoretically there is only one correct botanical name for any species of plant. This is the first published botanical name correctly assigned to it. However, synonyms often exist and sometimes persist, reflecting differences of opinion among botanists and technicalities that cannot be considered here.

The first word of the botanical name is the genus or general group to which a particular kind or species of plant belongs. The generic names are always capitalized. The second word designates the species and is the specific name. For example, the botanical name of the Smooth Wild Rose is *Rosa* (Latin for "rose") *blanda* (Latin for "smooth"). Botanical names used in this book agree, for the most part, with those in the *New Britton and Brown Illustrated Flora* and Gleason and Cronquist's *Manual*. Synonyms, original authors of the names, and related details can be found in these more technical books.

Other botanical works that deal with the names and ranges of plants have been consulted. These are listed in the references and include works by Morley, Monserud and Ownbey, Moore, Moore and Tryon, Lakela, Marie-Victorin, Fernald, and Scoggan.

Plant names, both common and botanical, often have interesting histories and may or may not describe the plant to which they are assigned. Linnaeus and other early botanists who gave botanical names to many of our plants were interested primarily in assigning distinctive names that were not in general use. For example, *Zizania*, the generic name of Wild Rice, was borrowed from "zizanion", the Greek word for the "tares" in New Testament parable. It is a distinctive name, but it does not describe Wild Rice. Other nomenclatural oddities, some mentioned in the text, include names borrowed from ancient mythology. *Heracleum* from Herakles and *Circaea* from Circe are examples.

Latin, it should be remembered, with a considerable borrowing from Greek, was once the language of science. Linnaeus (1707-1778) and those who followed him tried to describe each species of plant in a few Latin words and then selected 2 descriptive or distinctive words as the botanical name. This is the "binomial system."

In addition to the generic and specific names, "varieties" or even "forms" marking minor differences within a species may have Latin names. An example is our common variety of Canada Violet, *Viola canadensis* var. *rugulosa*.

Arrangement of Plants in This Book

Genera of plants that are basically similar and closely related are grouped into families such as the Rose Family and the Orchid Family. The families of flowering plants form 2 series: (1) Dicotyledonous plants (Dicots) which have 2 seed leaves, conspicuous flower parts typically in 4's and 5's, and usually net-veined leaves; and (2) Monocotyledonous plants (Monocots) which have 1 seed leaf, conspicuous flower parts usually in 3's, and usually parallel-veined leaves.

In this book the Dicots (Nos. 1 to 258) are placed first because some Dicots, such as those in the Crowfoot Family, are probably among the most primitive wild flowers. Many are also among the first to bloom in the spring. The Monocots (Nos. 259 to 300) follow, beginning with the Cattail Family and ending with the Orchid Family. Within the 2 series, the families are arranged in a general order of increasing complexity and specialization of flower structure. For example, Dicots with free, colored flower parts (petals and sometimes sepals) are Nos. 1 to 114. Dicots that generally have petals united, at least at the base, are Nos. 115 to 258.

Within the families, which are noted in the side headings, the species of wild flowers are placed in the genus (plural genera) to which they belong and under a heading in the text that gives both the common and the generic names. Thus all violets are under the heading "VIOLET (*Viola*)." Thereafter in the text the generic name "*Viola*" is usually abbreviated to "*V.*," the Yellow Violet (*Viola pubescens*) becoming *V. pubescens*.

It is generally accepted by botanists that a flower is a short stem or shoot, bearing several kinds of leaves modified to aid cross-pollination and the production of seeds. The floral leaves are of 4 kinds. Starting from the outside they are: sepals (forming the calyx), petals (forming the corolla), stamens which produce pollen, and the pistil or pistils which enclose ovules and later the seeds. The more primitive flowers have conspicuous flower parts (petals and sometimes sepals) that are free (not joined together) and somewhat leaf- or paddle-shaped.

6

Regular and irregular flowers. Pasque Flower (left) has regular flowers with free colored parts (as in Figure 4 of the chart on p. 9). Spotted Touch-me-not (right) has irregular flowers and free colored parts and a spur (as in Figure 7 of the chart).

In contrast, the more highly developed flowers have petals that are joined, at least at the base, and are often modified in shape or structure. Some kinds of plants have flower adaptations to facilitate pollination by wind and even water. Meadow Rue and Wild Rice are examples of wind-pollinated flowers.

Color of flowers is an obvious characteristic and a starting point for the appreciation of wild flowers. However, color is so variable, sometimes even within a single species, that the use of color alone as the basis for a logical and workable identification system is not practical. Those with yellow or pure white flowers are fairly constant, but nearly all other colored species occasionally have white (albino) flowers. These sometimes cross with the normal type to give intermediate shades. Most multicolored garden flowers originated in this way. Some kinds of wild flowers change color as they age. Examples are Large-flowered Trillium, which turns from white to pink, and the Virginia Bluebell, which is pink in bud but blue in full flower. The color photographs show the most usual color to the extent that it has been possible to reproduce it.

We suggest, therefore, that the reader look at the photographs to become familiar with the general shapes of the flowers and inflorescences of the various plant families and then use color, as illustrated, to help identify specific plants. Often color variations are noted in the text.

7

Aid to Identification of Wild Flowers

The key below and the chart on the facing page group most of the wild flowers in this book according to arrangement of flowers (inflorescence type) and characteristics of flower parts. Start with the key below. Choose the "A" statement that best fits the flower at hand. If the statement chosen has a figure number at the right, go to that figure on the chart for diagrammatic verification and identifying numbers of photographs of flowers of the same type. If there is no figure number (such as following "AAA"), proceed through subsequent letters of the alphabet until a figure number is reached.

Identification of Common Wild Flowers

  A. Flowers in umbels . . . . Figure 1
 AA. Flowers in heads . . . . Figure 2
AAA. Flowers otherwise arranged
      B. Flowers regular (symmetrical); no spurs
        C. Outer colored parts free (not joined together)
          D. 3 or 4 free, colored parts and same number of
            green parts . . . . Figure 3
        DD. 4 or more free, colored parts, but with *fewer*
            green than colored parts . . . . Figure 4
       DDD. 5 or more free, colored parts and *same number*
           of green parts . . . . Figure 5
       CC. Outer colored parts joined (fused), at least
         at base. . . . . Figure 6
     BB. Flowers irregular (asymmetrical); some with spurs.
      Colored parts free or fused . . . . Figure 7

❀❀❀❀❀❀❀❀❀❀❀❀❀

The key and chart include only flowers with colored (including white but not green) flower parts. Species with flower parts in 2's (Nos. 88 and 279) and those with small flowers in a spike, spadix, or spikelet (Nos. 259, 261-265) are not included. See Glossary (pp. 39-42) for unfamiliar terms.

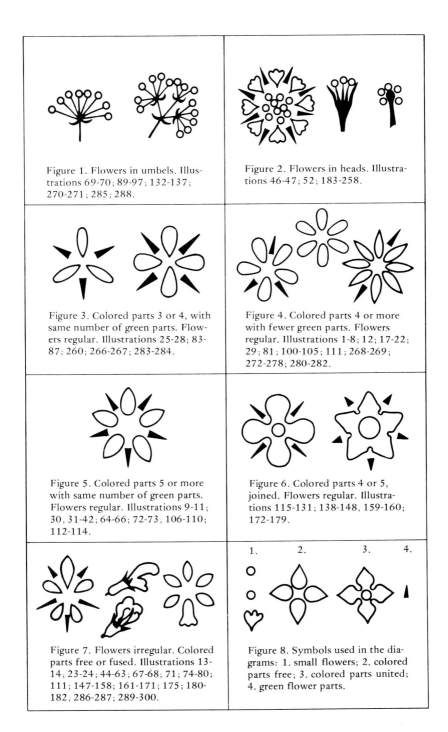

Figure 1. Flowers in umbels. Illustrations 69-70; 89-97; 132-137; 270-271; 285; 288.

Figure 2. Flowers in heads. Illustrations 46-47; 52; 183-258.

Figure 3. Colored parts 3 or 4, with same number of green parts. Flowers regular. Illustrations 25-28; 83-87; 260; 266-267; 283-284.

Figure 4. Colored parts 4 or more with fewer green parts. Flowers regular. Illustrations 1-8; 12; 17-22; 29; 81; 100-105; 111; 268-269; 272-278; 280-282.

Figure 5. Colored parts 5 or more with same number of green parts. Flowers regular. Illustrations 9-11; 30, 31-42; 64-66; 72-73, 106-110; 112-114.

Figure 6. Colored parts 4 or 5, joined. Flowers regular. Illustrations 115-131; 138-148, 159-160; 172-179.

Figure 7. Flowers irregular. Colored parts free or fused. Illustrations 13-14; 23-24; 44-63; 67-68; 71; 74-80; 111; 147-158; 161-171; 175; 180-182; 286-287; 289-300.

Figure 8. Symbols used in the diagrams: 1. small flowers; 2. colored parts free; 3. colored parts united; 4. green flower parts.

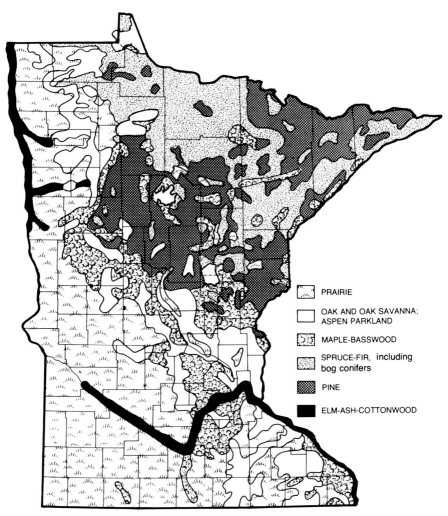

PRAIRIE

OAK AND OAK SAVANNA; ASPEN PARKLAND

MAPLE-BASSWOOD

SPRUCE-FIR, including bog conifers

PINE

ELM-ASH-COTTONWOOD

Presettlement vegetation types in Minnesota. (Adapted by Patricia Burwell from an unpublished map drawn by F. J. Marschner in 1930 for the United States Department of Agriculture, Washington, D.C.)

Where to Find Wild Flowers

Minnesota is a fine place to see and enjoy wild flowers. It is a botanical crossroads where 3 major vegetation types meet: the southern and eastern hardwood forests; the northern forest of pines, spruces, and other evergreens; and the western tall-grass prairies. Within these general vegetation types are many habitats characterized by specific groups of wild flowers and other plants.

The more extensive of these are: the central sand plain extending northward from Anoka to Brainerd; the much eroded limestone and sandstone country of the southeast; the rocky Lake Superior coast; the many bogs, marshes, and muskegs of the north including Big Bog near Red Lake; the scenic St. Croix and lower Mississippi river valleys; and the rocky prairies of the extreme southwestern counties.

Original boundaries of major vegetation types (see accompanying map) have been much modified by such human activities as farming, lumbering, and suppression of wild fires. But here and there remnants of the original vegetation can be found in forests, parks, wildlife areas, and along rights-of-way and water courses. Often it is the boundary transition areas or "edges" of vegetation types that are most favorable for wild flowers. Habitat disturbance, natural or man-made, favors many kinds of wild plants. Examples of such disturbed areas are: river bottoms flooded in early spring; sites of recent forest or prairie fires; and recently graded or brushed roadsides where herbicides have not been used extensively. To be successful, native plants with conspicuous flowers must grow where they can be seen easily and are available to insects. Areas of long-established vegetation, such as dense mature woods, sedge-covered marshes, and thick stands of tall prairie grasses often have fewer conspicuous wild flowers than do more open places.

Most wild flowers of European origin thrive best along roads, in old fields, pastures, and waste corners where the habitat has been modified by humans and domestic animals. These plants have long lived with humans and have been unwittingly selected by them during the long history of agriculture.

For finding wild flowers a good highway map is most helpful, especially one that shows state parks, larger state and federal wildlife management areas, and public forest lands. The most useful state maps also show larger streams and lakes and major railroad lines. Often where railroad and highway rights-of-way run side by side there is a strip of wild land that has never been broken, where native wild flowers remain and thrive. Several useful atlases of county maps drawn to a larger scale than the usual highway maps are available at booksellers, often as fishing and hunting guides. They frequently show smaller roads, other minor geographic features, and railroads.

All Minnesota state parks have hiking trails and the larger ones often have self-guiding nature trails as well as park naturalists in residence during the summer months. A statewide system of hiking, biking and snowmobile trails is being developed by the Minnesota Department of Natural Resources. Some of these are available for wild flower watching. There are also many fine county and city parks.

On the public lands of Minnesota and adjacent states and provinces wild flowers can be seen, enjoyed, and photographed, but they should not be picked or transplanted. Not only is this unwise and ecologically unsound, it is often illegal.

The Twin Cities Area

One can see and enjoy wild flowers in several excellent spots in the Twin Cities area.

The Eloise Butler Wild Flower Garden, founded by and named after a Minneapolis school teacher, is part of the Minneapolis Park System and is located near the western edge of the city. Here woodland, marsh, and prairie flowers, many identified with markers, can be seen from well-kept walking trails. A naturalist is on duty and public facilities are available. Dogs are not permitted. There is no admission charge.

Minnehaha Park, especially along Minnehaha Creek below the Falls, has interesting spring wild flowers. Here in seepage areas Skunk Cabbage blooms soon after the snow melts. Forget-me-not and Yellow Flag are also found here.

The University of Minnesota Landscape Arboretum near Chanhassen has fine trails through hardwood forest. A wide boardwalk crosses a bog, and naturalistic plantings of some of the less common wild flowers can be seen. Many shrubs, trees, vines, and garden plants are planted along several miles of winding roads. The beautiful headquarters building has a botanical library. The entrance fee or annual membership charge is well worth the price. Dogs must be leashed.

Carver Park, near Victoria, west of Lake Minnetonka, is one of several parks in the Hennepin County Park Reserve. Along its walking trails through woodlands, upland open areas, and swamps are many common wild flowers. Those who enjoy nature little modified find this an especially good hiking area. Many autumn composites — asters, goldenrod, and bonesets — grow here in the

The Big Woods of sugar maple, basswood, and oaks near Lake Minnetonka. Here some common wild flowers of spring are Hepatica, Bloodroot, Bellwort, Trillium, Blue Cohosh, and Yellow and Canada Violet. Later occasional blooming plants of Showy Orchid and Yellow Lady-slipper are found. Soils are clayey and fertile, much of the Big Woods is now rolling farmland. A good place to see this hardwood forest is the University of Minnesota Landscape Arboretum near Chanhassen. Chanhassen is the Siouan word for " sugar maple."

open areas. It is also a good spot for seeing water birds, including the rare trumpeter swans. In the fine headquarters building a naturalist can direct you to museum displays and educational programs. Admission is charged. Dogs are not permitted.

Southeastern Minnesota

In the hilly country of the southeast many of the most easily seen wild flower areas are literally "down in the valley." These valleys were wooded at the time of settlement and remain so. They have an abundance of spring wild flowers. Dry southwest-facing slopes on hills and bluffs, especially along the lower Mississippi River, are characterized by prairie plants. Such slopes are locally called "goat prairies." Most of the level uplands are in-

The last continental glaciers by-passed southeastern Minnesota, leaving deep valleys originally wooded with broad-leaved trees and prairielike uplands. On the slopes and riverbottoms are many wild flowers. Prairie flowers, such as the Grayheaded Coneflower shown here, add color to roadsides. In spring the river-bottom forests are blanketed with Virginia Bluebell, Trout Lily, and False Rue Anemone. Stream banks are carpeted with Ground Ivy.

tensely farmed. Only a few of the wild flower spots of the southeast can be mentioned here.

Frontenac State Park stands on the edge of the Mississippi River Valley and high above Lake Pepin. Although primarily a historic site, there are wooded trails, some of them steep, along which grow many kinds of wild flowers and ferns. State Highway 242 from Red Wing to the park follows an ancient valley containing woods and long swamps full of marsh vegetation. One of these marshes is within the park.

Of the several state parks farther south, our choices for spring wild flower enjoyment are: Carley, south of Plainview; Forestville, near Preston; and Lake Louise, near the Iowa border at Le Roy. All include river bottoms in which such wild flowers as False Rue Anemone, Virginia Bluebell, Swamp Buttercup, Dutchman's Breeches, White Trout Lily, Spring Beauty, and Missouri Violet grow. In spring the borders of streams, many of them trout streams, are carpeted with the blue flowers and mint-scented vines of Ground Ivy.

In backwaters, old channels, and oxbow lakes of the Mississippi River are extensive stands of Lotus Lily and Arrowhead. Partridge Pea and Flowering Spurge grow along roads. Near Northfield is Nerstrand Woods State Park, a rolling upland wooded area with streams and a waterfall. Wild flowers here are representative of

The last continental ice sheet melted about 10,000 years ago. Water accumulated along its edge forming several large lakes, now drained, and raised the level of glacial Lake Superior. From the lakes water flowed southward, cutting the wide valleys of the Minnesota, St. Croix, and lower Mississippi rivers. Today the wide bottoms of these ancient valleys are filled with marsh plants and floodplain trees. Marshes occupy undrained portions of the larger ancient lake basins. The photograph shows the Mississippi River bottoms near Winona. Here Lotus Lily (*Nelumbo*) and Broad-leaved Arrowhead are abundant.

the "Big Woods," a forest of sugar maple, basswood, and other broad-leaved trees that once covered much of south-central Minnesota. The fine display of spring wild flowers here includes Marsh Marigold in wetter areas.

Southern and Southwestern Minnesota

This area, now generally fertile farmland, was once prairie, except for the wooded stream and lake margins protected from

Much of southern and western Minnesota was originally tallgrass prairie. Early explorers from the forested East saw it as the edge of the "Great American Desert," but pioneer farmers found it fertile cropland. It was prairie both because less rain and snow fell here than in the forested regions and because prairie fires, often set by Indians, raged across it. Here, along roads and on the few unplowed prairie remnants, are tall grasses and many bright wild flowers such as Downy Phlox and Hoary Puccoon. Native legumes, such as Prairie Clover and Lead Plant, are common, and in summer and autumn there is a glorious assortment of Composites—goldenrod, sunflowers, asters, and blazing stars. The photograph is a September view along the Minnesota River not far from Shakopee.

In autumn the Big Woods is a mass of color: oranges and reds of maples, yellows of basswood, and purples and browns of oaks. Along roads the scarlet of sumac and the blues and purples of asters can be seen. In late summer yellow wands of Zigzag Goldenrod, patches of Woodland Sunflower, and Blue Wood Aster brighten forest edges.

prairie fires. Wild flower areas are now limited mostly to state parks, wildlife areas, and trails, and along rights-of-way, especially where highways and railroads are side by side. Often parks have preserved woods rather than prairie. The steep wooded lands in stream valleys were less suitable for farming than the prairies and were early valued as picnic spots by the prairie pioneers. Minneopa State Park near Mankato and Kilen Woods near Windom are examples of wooded valleys in prairie country. Both have trails along which are many wild flowers, especially in spring. At Minneopa there is a beautiful waterfall.

For typical prairie vegetation and wild flowers we suggest the rocky country of Rock and Pipestone counties in the extreme southwest. Blue Mounds State Park has a fine display of Prickly Pear Cactus that blooms about the first week in July. Here also can be seen the only Minnesota herd of bison. At Pipestone National Monument a fine self-guiding nature trail provides names of many of the prairie plants. Here also are the historic pipestone quarries and a fine museum emphasizing the aboriginal history of the area.

Farther north typical prairie vegetation of morainic areas can be seen at Lac Qui Parle State Park and the adjacent wildlife area, and at Big Stone Lake State Park. Big Stone Park also provides a fine view of the hills of South Dakota. At Glacial Lake State Park and along Glacial Lake State Trail which leads to it are many views of hilly prairie. The highway between Terrace and Sunberg is especially scenic with rolling hills and scattered, small lakes and potholes. Many late summer and autumn wild flowers, such as blazing stars, sunflowers, goldenrods, and asters, thrive here. Here also can be seen such native legumes as the Prairie Plum (*Astragalus crassicarpus*) with its low clusters of purple flowers in early spring and the Prairie Turnip (*Psoralea esculenta*) whose roots were a plant food of the Dakota Indians.

East-Central Minnesota

North of the Twin Cities and covering much of the area between the Mississippi and St. Croix rivers is a sandy plain laid down and leveled by the meandering Mississippi at the end of the last Ice Age. Here is much prairie vegetation and, where there have been no recent intense prairie fires, thin stands of oak (oak savanna) and aspen forest. Because the soil is sandy, vegetation is less

About 150 kinds of aquatic, shoreline, and marsh plants are found in Minnesota, not including those of northern bogs and muskegs. Some, such as the Yellow Water Lily, Arrowhead, Blue Flag, and Purple Loosestrife are conspicuous summer wild flowers. Others provide food and shelter for fishes, waterfowl, and other aquatic animals, large and small. One of the most interesting is Wild Rice, a native aquatic grass that has long been used by Indians. Its harvest and culture is now a minor industry in northern Minnesota.

dense than on the clayey prairies farther west. In late spring it is often gardenlike with a variety of bright flowers. Here can be seen Carolina Puccoon, Butterflyweed — both bright orange — Prairie Phlox, Western and Bracted Spiderwort, Large-flowered Penstemon, Pansy Violet, and Purple Avens. A good time to visit the sand plain is between June 1 and July 1.

Within this general area are the Mille Lacs Wildlife Area near Onamia, the Sherburne National Wildlife Refuge near Princeton, and Sand Dunes State Forest near Zimmerman. At the last park on old sand dunes and blowouts are found the plants that pioneer such unstable areas.

Near Onamia are several shallow Wild Rice lakes such as Lake Onamia along the main highway, which has long been harvested by Indians. Kathio State Park has both forest and open areas with representative wild flowers. Along the west shore of Mille Lacs Lake is one of the best spots in Minnesota to see Large-flowered Trillium, which blooms in spring. When in this area, do not miss the Indian Museum operated by the Minnesota Historical Society. It is near Vineland on the shore of Mille Lacs Lake and has some fine displays of Indian uses of wild plants.

East of the sand plain is the St. Croix River Valley with its rocky bluffs. Spring wild flowers are common in wooded areas along State Highway 95 running from Stillwater to the Interstate Park at Taylor's Falls. The latter location is near the northern limit of several kinds of southern and eastern wild flowers. On river bottoms is an open forest that is flooded each spring. Here in summer you can find Cardinal Flower and False Dragonhead. Summer wild flowers also flourish along State Highway 95.

Northeastern Minnesota

Duluth, on the southern edge of the northeastern Arrowhead Country, can be a base for several wild flower expeditions. Its fine system of city parks includes many wooded areas and ravines. Skyline Parkway traverses rocky areas high above the city. Minnesota Point, a long sandy spit extending into Lake Superior and enclosing the harbor, is well worth visiting. In the city park near the end of the point are plants typical of sandy Lake Superior beaches. Here Beach Pea is abundant. Jay Cooke State Park, a short drive from Duluth, contains a spectacular gorge along the St. Louis River. In the park there is a fine display of Large-flowered Trillium in spring.

Lake Superior somewhat moderates the climate along its coast, and along the North Shore several kinds of wild flowers may be seen that are less common or rare elsewhere in the state. Typical are Flowering Raspberry, with its spreading white flowers and maple-like leaves, and Tall Lungwort (locally called Bluebell). The latter has nodding, blue flowers and is a close relative of the Virginia Bluebell found in the southeast. Several European plants thrive here as wild flowers. Orange Hawkweed makes bright orange patches along roads and in clearings. Scentless Chamomile, Tansey, Common St. John's-wort, and Ox-eye Daisy all occur along roads. In some places plantings of Bird's-foot Trefoil and Crown Vetch in road cuts provide bright yellow and pink patches.

Lake Superior is the largest freshwater body in the world, and along its rugged coastline are many wild flowers, such as Flowering Raspberry and Tall Lungwort, not common elsewhere in Minnesota. Many low-growing wild flowers, e.g. Harebell and Three-tooth Cinquefoil, make natural rock gardens of cliffs and exposed headlands.

Split Rock Lighthouse State Park is an interesting place to stop. In addition to the marvelous view, one can see such rock plants as Common Bluebell, Three-tooth Cinquefoil, and Shrubby Cinquefoil. Growth of orange lichens on the rocks here is promoted by the droppings of gulls. Farther up the shore is Caribou Falls State Park. The trail, somewhat difficult to negotiate at its upper end, leads to one of Minnesota's most beautiful waterfalls. Along the trail are many of the characteristic forest plants and wild flowers of the region.

Inland in the Superior National Forest and the state forests are many stopping and camping places. The Boundary Waters Canoe Area and Isle Royale National Park in Lake Superior are good choices for an extended holiday. The latter can be reached by boat from Grand Portage. At Ely the U.S. Forest Service has a fine headquarters and museum. Those starting on canoe trips into the border wilderness must register here.

In the north, such as in Cass County where this photograph was
taken, pines—red, white, and jack—once covered much of the
landscape, and groves of these noble evergreens still characterize
it. The Red or "Norway" Pine is Minnesota's official state tree.
Beneath the pines on the sandy needle-covered forest floor, the
spring and early summer wild flowers include Fringed Polygala,
Stemless Lady-slipper, Twin Flower, Wood Anemone, Wintergreen, and False Lily-of-the-Valley.

Forest fires followed logging of the pines at the turn of the century. After the fires a wealth of purple Fireweed and other robust herbs came in on the burned area. These in turn were replaced by brush and second-growth forest, largely of aspen. The herbs and shrubs fed a multitude of deer. This forest, now mature, supplies much pulp wood and other forest products. Large-leaf Aster, Lindley's Aster, and Wild Sarsaparilla are common summer and autumn wild flowers here. Goldenrod and sunflowers brighten roadsides in the fall.

North-Central Minnesota

Much of this rolling forested country was originally covered with white and red pine that fell under the logger's axe, but scattered stands of magnificent pine remain, especially in Cass, Itasca, and Hubbard counties. Here such typical northern forest plants as Large-leaf Aster, Lindley's Aster, and Wild Sarsaparilla are abundant. Fireweed and Pearly Everlasting are common in old fields and openings, and Ox-eye Daisy and Tall Buttercup grow along open roadsides and in pastures.

There are many grassy and mossy bogs and marshes. Such oddities as Pitcher Plant and Sundew (both insectivorous), a variety of shrubs of the Heath Family, and some low plants that range northward into subarctic and arctic regions grow in these habitats. Remember that bogs and "muskegs" (as the wooded bogs are called) are hard going. They can be dangerous and are the homes of myriad mosquitoes. Those who wish to see some of the bog plants without too great an effort might try Dr. Robert's Na-

Within the northern upland forest are many swamps, bogs, and muskegs, the muskegs wooded with black spruce, tamarack, and white cedar. The low-growing vegetation is largely sedges and evergreen shrubs of the Heath Family. In the mossy muskegs are found native orchids and many kinds of wild flowers and other plants typical of more northern regions. This photograph shows an open marsh of heath shrubs with Cotton Grass (*Eriophorum*) in the foreground and a wooded muskeg behind. Cotton Grass is really a kind of sedge with many white, tassellike spikes. The insectivorous Pitcher Plant also grows here.

ture Trail near Douglas Lodge in Itasca Park. Many hiking trails and roads traverse the park. However, Itasca is often crowded. If you are camping, we suggest you use other fairly close park and forest campgrounds.

Northwestern Minnesota

Few lakes are found in extreme western and northwestern Minnesota. Much of this area is within the basin of a very large ancient lake — Glacial Lake Agassiz — that was impounded and then drained naturally at the end of the last Ice Age. Here are the "Big Bog," the Red Lake Indian Reservation and in the Red River Valley much level farmland that was originally low prairie. An interesting trip through a vast area of level peat land could start at Redby or Red Lake on Lower Red Lake. Follow the Great River Road (Highways 1 and 89) to the Agassiz National Wildlife Refuge and the Thief Lake Wildlife Area. Moose and many kinds of waterfowl are found here as well as an abundance of marsh plants and summer and autumn wild flowers.

In the Red River Valley the main highways and the railroads that usually parallel them often run in a north-south direction. They follow the ancient beach lines of Glacial Lake Agassiz, and abundant and diverse prairie wild flowers often grow on the sandy and gravelly soil of these beaches. Toward the southern end of this ancient lake basin near Moorhead is Buffalo River State Park in which many kinds of prairie plants can be seen, including White Lady-slipper in early summer. Eastward, near Detroit Lakes, are many Wild Rice stands; some of the most accessible are in the Tamarac National Wildlife Refuge. Wild Rice is hand harvested here about September 1.

Wild Flowers and the Calendar

In Minnesota some wild flowers are in bloom throughout the growing season. However, most can be grouped, somewhat arbitrarily, into spring, summer, and autumn flowering kinds. These floral seasons correspond only approximately to the calendar seasons and for the Twin Cities region can be dated about as follows:

Spring, from about April 15 to June 15, with a peak around May 15. Among the first spring wild flowers to bloom are Skunk Cabbage, Hepatica, Pasque Flower, and Bloodroot.

Summer, from about June 16 to August 15, with a peak bloom around July 15. Typical of this period are Butterflyweed, Indian Paint Brush, Brown-eyed Susan, Ox-eye Daisy, Grayheaded Coneflower, and Prairie Clover.

Autumn, from about August 16 to killing frost (usually around October 5), with a peak bloom about September 10. Characteristic of the autumn blooming season are asters, goldenrods, blazing stars, sunflowers, Joe-pye weed, and gentians.

Minnesota is about 400 miles long from south to north. Spring usually comes 4 or 5 days earlier in the southeast than in the Twin Cities area. The last killing frost of spring may be expected about a week later along Lake Superior than in the Twin Cities area and 3 to 4 weeks later in the Boundary Waters Canoe area. The growing season is about 160 days in the extreme southeast, 155 days in the Twin Cities area, and 100 days or even less along the northern border. The onset of spring, as shown by observations of plant development, varies considerably in different years and for different kinds of plants. Spring development of some common kinds of forest trees is usually 15 to 20 days earlier at St. Paul than at Ely.

The following list of approximate dates of flowering periods may be useful in planning trips to see wild flowers:

Skunk Cabbage (Twin Cities)	4/10-5/10
Early woodland wild flowers (southeast)	4/10-5/1
Early woodland wild flowers (Twin Cities)	4/15-5/15
Early prairie wild flowers, especially Pasque Flower (south and southwest)	4/15-5/15
Late prairie wild flowers (central sand plain)	6/1-7/1
Prickly Pear Cactus (southwest)	7/1-15
Summer roadside wild flowers (central and north)	7/15-30
Muskeg and bog wild flowers (north)	6/20-7/15
North Shore wild flowers, especially Flowering Raspberry and Tall Lungwort	7/1-15
Summer prairie wild flowers (south and east)	7/15-8/15
Floodplain wild flowers along St. Croix River	8/1-30
Lotus Lilies at Lake Minnetonka	8/10-20
Summer wild flowers (Twin Cities)	7/15-8/15
Autumn wild flowers (southern and western prairies)	8/1-frost
Autumn wild flowers (northern forest)	8/1-frost
Wild Rice harvest (northern counties)	8/25-9/5

Indians and Wild Plants

The Indians of the forests and prairies that are now Minnesota and adjacent areas had names and uses for many of the plants considered here as wild flowers. From these and other plants they obtained food, fiber, construction material, medicines, and items having artistic, magical, and religious uses. Some of these values

26

and uses are referred to elsewhere in this book, and sources of additional information may be found in the references.

The Chippewas of Lake Superior marked the progress of the year by "moons," six of which were named for changes in the vegetation. They were:

Flower Moon	May
Strawberry Moon	June
Raspberry Moon	July
Blueberry Moon	August
Wild Rice Moon	September
Falling Leaf Moon	October

The Chippewas knew plants and in their language grouped those that were similar in general appearance or use. According to Edwin James, an early physician and traveler interested in plants, Indians, and Indian languages, the Chippewa classification of the green world was generally as follows:

A. Meti-goag	Woody plants
B. Shingobeek	Evergreens
BB. Ne-bi-shun	Broad-leaved trees and shrubs
AA. Weah-gush-kean	Herbaceous (nonwoody) plants
B. Me-zhus-keen	Grasslike plants
BB. Other kinds	

Plants with edible berries or fruits were also grouped, the Chippewa names for these often including "min" or "meen" meaning "berry." Some examples are: manomin (wild rice, literally "good berry"), o-da-na-me-na (strawberry, literally "heart berry") and menagha or meen (blue berry).

Berries were eaten in season or dried for winter use on rocks or on frames covered with grass or rush mats. Dried berries were often added to dried meat and fat to make pemmican used in traveling or as a condensed winter food. The pulp of wild plums was dried after being boiled with maple sugar to form a "leathery substance" that in winter was stewed with dried meat.

Plants producing starchy foods were especially valued. Of these wild rice was the most important. Many Indian villages were located on wild rice stands, and battles were fought between the Dakota (Sioux) and Chippewa Indians for control of such sites. Harvesting and processing this native grain involved several complicated steps and was a triumph of primitive technology. The grain was gathered, dried, parched, threshed, and winnowed before it could be stored indefinitely for food.

On the prairies the principal starchy food was the Prairie Turnip (*Psoralea esculenta*). This legume, which has a thick root somewhat like a small turnip, was dug, cooked like a common potato, and the central starchy part eaten. Lycurgus Moyer, a pioneer judge at Montevideo and an excellent botanist, noted that campsites of traveling bands of Dakota were often marked by piles of used roots. This plant is now scarce and found only on unplowed prairie remnants.

Arrowhead (*Sagittaria*) tubers were removed from the soft bottoms of shallow lakes and streams by treading the mud with bare feet; the tubers then floated to the surface. They are starchy and much like a small potato, but less firm. The Chippewas strung and dried these "swan potatoes" and added them to winter stews. Groundnut (*Apios*), a legume with underground chains of tubers ranging from marble-size to 3 inches in diameter, were used by the Menomini in Wisconsin. The tubers were peeled, parboiled, sliced, and dried for winter use. Groundnut was early imported into Europe as a possible crop plant, but cultivation proved impractical because the tubers take several years to develop. The fleshy roots of Pondlily and Lotus were also sometimes eaten by Indians.

Another American plant that was sent to Europe as a possible food is the Jerusalem Artichoke. This wide-leaved perennial sunflower is quite common on open prairies and sometimes along roads. Its edible tubers which look much like small knobby potatoes were used by Indians who sometimes cultivated the plant. Jerusalem Artichoke was imported into Europe around 1600, about the same time as the common potato. It never gained much favor, even though the French explorer Samuel de Champlain thought the tubers tasted like artichoke. "Jerusalem" is the result of linguistic confusion. "Girasol," literally "turning to the sun," was the name given it in Spain. When imported into England "girasol" became "Jerusalem."

Several wild plants were used for flavoring in Indian cooking. Examples are Wild Onions and Wild Ginger. According to Frances Densmore, who early in this century gathered much information on plants valued by the Chippewa Indians, tea was often brewed by the Chippewa to avoid drinking raw water when traveling. Tea was made from the leaves of plants, including Labrador Tea, Wintergreen, and Red Raspberry. The flowers of various wild plants were also collected throughout the summer, dried, and used later for tea sweetened with maple sugar.

Many of the plants considered here as wild flowers were highly regarded by the Indians for their medicinal properties. For the most part such plants have herbage or roots with a strong odor, disagreeable taste, milky or colored juice, and drastic, even poisonous, properties. Many were also used by white settlers and early physicians and a few are still used. Frances Densmore lists 69 medicinal plants used by both Indians and whites. Among them are Yarrow, Sweet Flag, Wintergreen, Labrador Tea, Cup Plant, Culver's Root, Boneset, Blue Cohosh, Baneberry, Bloodroot, and Milkweed.

Often the roots were collected, dried, and stored in special medicine bags. Knowledge of medicinal plants was part of the Indian culture and was based largely on generations of practical experience. However, the medicinal or magical properties were sometimes revealed in dreams. Among the Chippewa, information on identification and application of medicinal plants was passed down to initiates and members of the Midewiwin Lodge to which many males belonged. Often the medicinemen who dispensed medicinal herbs specialized in only a few kinds. Information on other herbs was sometimes purchased by one medicineman from another. Like the present-day physician, the Indian medicineman charged patients for specialized knowledge and services rendered.

Medicine in Indian culture was not sharply separated from magic or even music. Roots were thought to be especially potent both because they obtained strength from the earth and because they were dug by the bear, an animal they especially revered.

Indian Hemp and its close relative Dogbane have a thin but tough fibrous bark. This was "spun" into cordage, twine, and thread by rolling it against the thigh with the palm of the hand and was used for bow strings and fish nets. Mats were made from leaves of cattails and stems of bulrushes, first softened by boiling, then dried and woven or plaited when dampened and pliable. Cattail down was used as disposable diaper material, packed around the infant on the cradle board and often mixed with dry sphagnum moss and punky wood. The down was also stuffed inside moccasins for winter warmth.

Wild Flower Immigrants

Many of our roadside wild flowers of summer are naturalized Americans. They came as immigrants, mostly from Europe, some from gardens and dooryards, some as crop and drug plants, and some, uninvited and unwanted, as weeds to follow and plague the farmer. Common examples are Sow Thistle, Creeping Jenny, Field Thistle, Leafy Spurge, and Dandelion.

Below is a sampling by color of the more respected plant immigrants brought from foreign gardens and dooryards to new homes here. These plants later escaped to roadsides, fields, and waste corners where they can still be found. They may be used to recreate flower and herb gardens of the 1800s, with some vigorous hoeing now and then to keep them in their place.

Yellow	Butter-and-Eggs, Moneywort, Tansy, Yellow Flag, Costmary, Cypress Spurge
Blue and Purple	European Bellflower, Ground Ivy, Chicory, Sweet Rocket, Catnip
White	Yarrow, Ox-eye Daisy, Jack-by-the-Hedge (*Alliaria*), Common Valerian
Pink	Bouncing Bet
Orange	Tawny Day Lily

The trailing and low-growing plants, such as Ground Ivy, Moneywort, and Cypress Spurge, were often planted on graves and still can be found in old cemeteries.

Eating Wild Flowers — Don't!

Wild flowers are to be seen and, along with other wild plants, are usually not to be eaten. The safe approach is not to eat any wild plant or any part of it unless you are certain of its identification and edibility. The idea that wild plants provide a natural smorgasbord of delicacies that can be gathered and eaten with impunity is both fallacious and dangerous. Many wild plants are poisonous. Indians and country people have long been aware of this.

Part of the long history of plants is their development of means to avoid being eaten by insects and other herbivores.

Plants have many obvious survival stratagems such as thorns, spines, harsh leaves, and woodiness. Plants also produce and store a wide variety of protective organic chemicals. These range in properties from objectionable taste to very poisonous. Toxicity often depends upon the kind of animal that eats the plant and is sometimes quite specific. It is likely that any plant readily available and palatable to all kinds of herbivores would not long survive.

Plants that are poisonous or have other drastic or unpleasant effects on humans and their domestic animals are widely distributed in the plant kingdom. They are especially common in the Crowfoot, Parsley, Lobelia, Milkweed, Dogbane, Barberry, Poppy, Nightshade, Arum, Iris, and Lily families. The unpalatability of others, such as Locoweed in the Bean Family and Common Wormwood and Ironweed in the Composite Family, ensures that they will thrive in overgrazed pastures. One of the most interesting cases of differential toxicity is Common St. John's-wort, which is toxic to light-colored but not to dark-colored grazing animals. It is a matter of increasing the light-sensitivity of the skin.

Often objectionable substances are more concentrated in the roots than in other plant parts, and roots have long been used as a source of medicinal drugs. Eating roots of wild plants is especially chancy. Children have died from eating a small piece of Water Hemlock root.

For more information on this subject see the books by Muenscher, Kingsbury, and by Fernald and Kinsey. These are listed in the references.

Wild Flowers in the Garden

This is not a treatise on horticulture, but since many wild flowers are available from nurseries and seed companies, a few comments on wild flower culture may be useful.

In general wild flowers that are natives of other areas, especially of Eurasia, and have become naturalized along roads and in other places present few cultural difficulties. Often they were originally garden plants or came as colorful stowaways and, as previously indicated, thrive with little care. We refer to plants like Bouncing Bet, Tawny Day Lily, Butter-and-Eggs, Sweet Rocket, Ground Ivy, Ox-eye Daisy, Tansy, and European Bellflower. The

31

principal difficulty is keeping them under control. They tend to be weedy but, in their own fashion, are quite ornamental. Even Creeping Jenny, which has had a bad press and is more politely called Field Bindweed, makes an attractive plant in an outdoor hanging basket. Raising native wild flowers, however, is more difficult. Many are fussy about soil chemistry, especially alkalinity or acidity (pH), and have quite specific requirements for soil moisture and shade. Since each is different, the only general rule is the rule-of-thumb that they grow best under conditions similar to those in which you see them in the wild. Bog plants thrive in bogs, prairie plants in prairie conditions, and woodland flowers in shady places.

Some of the most successful native kinds in our shady dooryard at Minnetonka, where the soil is quite limy, have been Wood Phlox, Canada Violet, and Star-flowered False Solomon's Seal. Harebell is easily grown in the rockery, as is Meadow Violet. Virginia Bluebell does well with daffodils in moister spots. We have been unsuccessful with plants that thrive in acid sandy areas — such as Carolina Puccoon, Butterflyweed, and Pansy Violet. By contrast, Bracted Spiderwort, which often grows on sandy, acid soil, does well and is very showy.

Lady-slippers, now available from some nurseries, require special·care and stable situations where they can remain undisturbed for many years. The Stemless Lady-slipper requires acid soil, but the Pink-and-White and Yellow Lady-slippers require soil that is neutral to somewhat alkaline. Field mice can be troublesome in winter because they eat the underground parts. In general, raising lady-slippers is too uncertain for most amateur gardeners, and we conclude it is better to enjoy these plants in the wild. False Dragonhead (*Physostegia*) and Cardinal Flower are showy wild flowers that can be bought from nurseries. The former does well in the perennial garden if given plenty of water, and the latter practically requires wet feet. New England Aster is easily grown and makes a robust, colorful garden plant that flowers from late summer until frost.

Transplanting spring woodland wild flowers is usually futile, especially when the flowers are in bloom. Even as they bloom, these plants are storing food and forming new underground parts. The stored food is necessary for growth the next spring. If you transplant a Trillium in bloom, you will probably kill it. The same is true of lilies and many other wild plants. Some wild flowers, such as Pasque Flower and Virginia Bluebell, are easily raised from seed.

A useful book on growing native wild flowers is *Pioneering with Wild Flowers* by George D. Aiken, retired U.S. Senator from Vermont, where for many years he has operated a wild flower nursery. Catalogues of wild flower nurseries also supply much helpful cultural advice.

Conservation of Wild Flowers

Early explorers and settlers often viewed wild flowers as part of a landscape destined to be reshaped by plow and axe; wheat and corn lands were needed and logs and lumber for building. There were exceptions. Some plants were used as medicinal herbs and spring greens. Children gathered spring flowers for May baskets and one prairie farm wife, probably reflecting the sentiments of many, noted in a diary that she admired the prairie wild flowers but "supposed it was sinful." Some early explorers, especially S. H. Long and J. N. Nicollet, collected plant specimens and sent them east to such botanical savants as Asa Gray and John Torrey. Others published lists and catalogues of native plants they had found.

The first attempt at a complete catalogue of Minnesota higher plants was made by Warren Upham, who published a list of 1650 kinds (species and varieties) in 1883. Of these, 1582 were flowering plants. This list was published by the Minnesota Geological and Natural History Survey and included records of earlier botanists, some of them school teachers. Upham first mapped the boundary between the wooded region and the prairie in Minnesota, while driving along the edge with a horse and buggy.

However, official interest in Minnesota flora — except, of course, for the pines that fed the sawmills — developed only near the end of the century. In 1889, 1890, and 1891 the legislature sponsored, as part of the Geological and Natural History Survey of Minnesota, a botanical survey of the state. The work was done under the direction of Conway MacMillan then professor of botany at the University of Minnesota. The resulting report is a thick, technical volume entitled *The Metaspermae of the Minnesota Val-*

ley. In it can be found all that was known about Minnesota plants up to that time, including a list of earlier publications. MacMillan also wrote a less technical book entitled *Minnesota Plant Life,* published in 1899.

The Pink-and-White or Showy Lady-slipper achieved its status as the official Minnesota state flower or "floral emblem" only after botanical and legal difficulties. The confusion occurred because 6 different species of lady-slipper orchids grow in Minnesota. In 1892 plans were made for a Minnesota exhibit for the World's Fair at Chicago — the famous Columbian Exposition. Before that time, Minnesota had no official flower. Accounts of what happened differ, but apparently the Women's Auxiliary of the Board of Fair Managers urged the legislature to adopt as a floral emblem the Wild Lady-slipper or Moccasin Flower, *Cypripedium calceolus.* The legislature did that and the 1893 Legislative Manual or Blue Book has a rather poor illustration, probably of the Pink-and-White Lady-slipper, with a caption noting that 6 kinds of lady-slippers grow in Minnesota. But errors and uncertainties had crept in. First, the true Moccasin Flower, although a lady-slipper, has leafless stems and rosy flowers and is not the more robust Pink-and-White. Second, the botanical name recommended is that of the European Yellow Lady-slipper. Minnesota's two yellow kinds, the Small Yellow and the Large Yellow Lady-slipper, are often considered to be varieties of this species. To confuse matters further, the lady-slipper on the state flag was white and many of the early Blue Books picture a bouquet of lady-slippers of assorted colors.

Nearly 10 years of lady-slipper confusion went by, and then in 1902 the ladies of the St. Anthony Study Circle straightened it out and, through Mrs. E. C. Chatfield of Minneapolis, persuaded the legislature to modify the statutes so that there was no doubt about the identity of the Minnesota state flower. It was designated, and has remained, the Pink-and-White Lady-slipper.

The first public wild flower garden in Minnesota, now called the Eloise Butler Wild Flower Garden, was established in Glenwood Park, Minneapolis, in 1907. In an account of its establishment in the Proceedings of the Minnesota Academy of Science for 1910, Miss Butler noted that "teachers of botany and other interested citizens petitioned the Park Board to set aside a tract of land for a wild, botanic garden." It was opened to the public on

April 20, 1907, a historic date for wild flower conservation and appreciation. Miss Butler taught botany in Minneapolis schools and had a special interest in algae as well as in wild flowers.

As the population of Minnesota increased, concern grew for some of the rarer and more colorful wild flowers. Unrestricted picking, especially of flowers for sale, was causing some kinds to become scarce. Therefore in 1925 the legislature passed a protective law "The Conservation of Certain Wildflowers" (Minn. Statute 17.23). This law with amendments made in 1935 prohibits the taking, buying, and selling of lady-slippers and other orchids, trilliums, lilies, gentians, arbutus, and lotus from public lands without permission of the Minnesota Comissioner of Agriculture and from private lands without permission of both the landowner and the commissioner. The protected wild flowers "may not be dug, cut, plucked, pulled, or gathered in any manner." Violation is a misdemeanor and fine or imprisonment is the penalty.

The law was helpful, at least in the Minnetonka area. Yellow Lady-slippers, which, according to older residents, nearly disappeared early in this century, returned to become moderately abundant in hardwood forests. Unfortunately they are again becoming scarce because of land development.

It should be emphasized that other restrictions on taking wild flowers and other plants from public lands, such as forests, parks, and wildlife areas are in force. Information can be obtained from the local land manager. For example, in state parks it is illegal to take plants or plant parts of any kind.

In addition to legal protection and preservation, some management of suitable habitats is often essential. Prairie plants, for example, may benefit from occasional burning over of the area or from moderate grazing, both of which simulate original prairie conditions. Water must be retained in bogs and marshes. In forested areas some kinds of wild flowers are favored by cutting of trees and brush but others are not. Yellow and Showy Lady-slippers, for instance, are forest plants but thrive best in open forests where they are not shaded out by dense growth of trees and brush.

In Minnesota about one-fourth of the land is in public ownership, but this land is mostly in the northern forested area. Here there is ample space for wild flowers. However, in the south and west the original prairies are now mostly farmland. Here some parcels of undisturbed lands, especially low-lying wetlands, have been preserved for waterfowl and other wildlife, largely through the efforts of state and federal agencies and financed by sportsmen's money. Recently the state, under the Division of Parks, has also established programs for preserving very valuable scientific and natural areas, and acquiring and developing lands for trails, some of which are on abandoned railroad grades. Both programs benefit wild flowers and provide opportunities for seeing them.

Privately financed organizations of natural history enthusiasts and others who are ecologically minded have also done much for wild flowers. The Minnesota Chapter of the Nature Conservancy has acquired and permanently preserved about 50 choice natural areas, incuding 25 remnants of unbroken upland prairie. This nonprofit organization deserves the support of those interested in wild flowers. Other organizations that have helped and still are helping to preserve our wild flower heritage are the Minnesota Academy of Science, the Audubon Society, the Minnesota Horticultural Society, the Minnesota Garden Clubs, and the Minnesota Ornithologists' Union. The efforts, interest, and generosity of private and corporate landowners should also be recognized. Some of the better undisturbed natural areas now remain only because someone had the foresight and appreciation to leave them undisturbed as pieces of yesterday's landscape to be enjoyed today and tomorrow—and also were willing to make the effort to preserve them *now*.

References

Systematics and Plant Distribution: Regional

Britton, N. L. and A. Brown. 1913. *An Illustrated Flora of the Northern United States, Canada and the British Possessions.* 3 vols. New York: Scribner.

Curtis, J. T. 1959. *The Vegetation of Wisconsin.* Madison: University of Wisconsin Press.

Fernald, M. L. 1950. *Gray's Manual of Botany.* 8th ed. New York: American Book Co.

Gleason, H. A. 1952. *The New Britton and Brown Illustrated Flora of the Northeastern United States and Canada.* 3 vols. New York: Hafner.

Gleason, H. A. and A. Cronquist. 1963. *Manual of Vascular Plants of Northeastern United States and Adjacent Canada.* New York: Van Nostrand.

Marie-Victorin, F. 1947. *Flore Laurentienne*. Montreal: Les Frères des Écoles Chrétienne.

Rydberg, P. A. 1932. *Flora of the Prairies and Plains of Central North America*. New York: New York Botanical Garden.

Scoggan, H. J. 1957. *Flora of Manitoba*. Bulletin 140. National Museum of Canada. Ottawa.

Stevens, O. A. 1933. *Wild Flowers of North Dakota*. Bulletin 269. North Dakota Agricultural Experiment Station. Fargo.

Systematics and Plant Distribution: Minnesota

Lakela, O. 1965. *A Flora of Northeastern Minnesota*. Minneapolis: University of Minnesota Press.

MacMillan, C. 1892. *The Metaspermae of the Minnesota Valley*. Report of the Minnesota Geological and Natural History Survey of Minnesota. Botanical Series I. Minneapolis: Harrison-Smith.

MacMillan, C. 1899. *Minnesota Plant Life*. Report of the Minnesota Geological and Natural History Survey. Botanical Series III. St. Paul.

Monserud, W. and G. B. Ownbey. 1971. *Common Wild Flowers of Minnesota*. Minneapolis: University of Minnesota Press.

Moore, J. W. 1973. A catalogue of the flora of Cedar Creek Natural History Area, Anoka and Isanti Counties, Minnesota. *Bulletin of the Museum of Natural History, University of Minnesota*. Occasional Paper No. 12. Minneapolis.

Moore, J. W. and R. M. Tryon Jr. 1946. *A Preliminary Checklist of the Flowering Plants, Ferns and Fern Allies of Minnesota*. Department of Botany, University of Minnesota, Minneapolis.

Morley, T. 1966. *Spring Flora of Minnesota*. Department of Botany, University of Minnesota, Minneapolis.

Moyer, L. R. 1910. The prairie flora of southwestern Minnesota. *Bulletin of the Minnesota Academy of Science for 1910*, pp. 68-92.

Moyle, J. B. 1964. *Northern Non-woody Plants* 3rd ed. Minneapolis: Burgess.

Moyle, J. B. and N. Hotchkiss. 1945. The aquatic and marsh vegetation of Minnesota and its value to waterfowl. *Minnesota Department of Conservation Technical Bulletin* 3. St. Paul.

Rosendahl, C. O. and A. Cronquist. 1945. The goldenrods of Minnesota: a floristic study. *American Midland Naturalist* 33: 244-253. Jan.

Rosendahl, C. O. and A. Cronquist. 1949. The asters of Minnesota: a floristic study. *American Midland Naturalist* 42:502-512. Sept.

Russell, N. H. 1957-1958. The violets of Minnesota. *Proceedings of the Minnesota Academy of Science* 25-26:126-199.

Upham, Warren. 1884. Catalogue of the flora of Minnesota, including its phanerogamous and vascular cryptogamous plants indigenous, naturalized, and adventitive. Part VI. *Annual Report for 1883 of the Minnesota Geological and Natural History Survey.*

Ethnobotany

Densmore, F. 1928. Uses of plants by the Chippewa Indians. *44th Annual Report of the Bureau of American Ethnology,* pp. 274-347. Republished by Dover Publications, New York, 1974, under the title: *How Indians Use Wild Plants for Food, Medicine, and Crafts.*

Hovgaard, W. 1914. *The Voyages of the Norsemen to North America.* New York: the American-Scandinavian Foundation.

James, E. 1830. *A Narrative of the Captivity and Adventures of John Tanner.* . . . New York. Reprinted in 1956 by Ross and Haines, Minneapolis.

Kohl, J. G. 1860. *Kitchi-Gami. Wandering around Lake Superior.* London. Reprinted in 1956 by Ross and Haines, Minneapolis.

Musil, F. 1972. Ponca cures. *Nebraskaland* 50:18-19, 60-61.

Smith, H. H. 1923. Ethnobotany of the Menomini Indians. *Bulletin of Public Museum of Milwaukee* 4.

Others

Aiken, G. D. 1969. *Pioneering with Wild Flowers.* New York: Prentice-Hall.

Birdseye, C. and E. G. Birdseye. 1951. *Growing Woodland Plants.* London: Oxford University Press. Reprinted in 1972 by Dover Publications, New York.

Fernald, M. L. and A. C. Kinsey. 1958. *Edible Wild Plants of Eastern North America.* New York: Harper.

Gilbert, J. 1974. Nature's calendar. *Minnesota Horticulturist* 102: 61.

Hodson, A. C. 1951. How go the seasons? *Minnesota Farm and Home Science* 8:15. Feb.

Kenfield, W. G. 1966. *The Wild Garden in the Wild Landscape. The Art of Naturalistic Landscaping.* New York: Hafner.

Kingsbury, J. M. 1964. *Poisonous Plants of the United States and Canada*. Englewood Cliffs, N.J.: Prentice-Hall.

Moyle, J. B. 1944. Wild rice in Minnesota. *Journal of Wildlife Management* 8:177-184.

Muenscher, W. C. 1939. *Poisonous Plants of the United States*. New York: Macmillan. Reprinted in 1975 by Collier Books, New York.

Phillips, E. P. 1943. *Beekeeping*. New York: Macmillan.

Stark, O. J. 1974. A natural wild garden built by order. *American Horticulturist* 59:4-12.

Stevens, O. A. 1933. Poisonous plants and plant products. *North Dakota Agricultural Experiment Station Bulletin* 265:30.

Watson, B. F. 1975. *Minnesota and Environs Weather Almanac 1976*. Navarre, Minn.: Freshwater Biological and Research Foundation.

Glossary

Achene.	A dry, seedlike fruit.
Acrid.	Having a sharp burning or biting taste.
Alternate.	With a single leaf at a stem node.
Annual.	Completes life cycle in 1 year.
Arching.	With tip bent backward or outward.
Ascending.	With tip rising and not bent backward.
Awn.	A bristlelike structure, especially on a grass spikelet.
Axil.	The inside angle of the junction of leaf and stem.
Balsamic.	A sweet, aromatic, somewhat resinous odor.
Basal.	Rising directly from underground parts; usually refers to leaves.
Biennial.	Completes life cycle in 2 years.
Blade.	The part of a leaf or leaflet above the stalk.
Bract.	A small, leaflike structure below a flower; see also Involucre.
Bulb.	A short, underground stem covered with scaly leaves; like an onion.
Calyx.	The outermost or lowermost series of flower parts, often green; made up of sepals.
Capsule.	A dry fruit containing seeds; a pod.
Clasping.	Referring to a leaf base that goes all or partly around the stem.

Compound.	Having several similar parts or arrangements, as a compound leaf with leaflets or a compound umbel.
Corm.	The thick, underground portion of a stem, usually rounded and often somewhat flattened.
Corolla.	The series of flower parts second from the bottom or the outside of a flower; usually colored; made up of petals.
Cultivar.	A variety of plant selected by horticulturists; usually not persisting in the wild.
Cut.	Refers to leaves with margins deeply divided into narrow, often irregular segments.
Disk.	The central portion of some flower heads, such as sunflowers and asters; may be flat or raised.
Divided.	Separated into distinct, often narrow segments, as in some leaves.
Filament.	The stalk of a stamen, usually slender.
Flower head.	See Head.
Follicle.	An elongate pod opening along 1 edge to release seeds.
Free.	Not attached to other parts.
Fruit.	Seed or seeds with attached or enclosing parts; may be dry or fleshy.
Fused.	With parts grown together.
Glabrous.	Without hairs.
Gland.	A cell filled with resin, oil, or other substance; may be stalked or make a semitransparent or dark dot in the leaf blade.
Haustorium.	An elongate structure, usually short and somewhat rootlike, whereby a dodder penetrates the stems of other plants. (See "dodder" in the index.)
Head.	A compact inflorescence of essentially stalkless flowers.
Herbage.	Stems and leaves considered together.
Inflorescence.	The flowering part of a plant.
Involucre.	Applied to a head in the Composite Family; a series of reduced leaves (bracts) enclosing or surrounding the flowers in the head.

40

Irregular.	Flower parts other than regular; see Regular. Includes flowers with 2 lips, bilateral symmetry, spurs, or parts of markedly different sizes or with nonsymmetrical arrangements.
Lobed.	In leaves, the wide divisions of the margin, extending more than halfway to the center of the blade.
Midrib.	The central vein of a pinnately veined leaf.
Nerves.	The principal veins running the length of a leaf blade; counts of nerves may include the midrib — as in 3-nerved.
Node.	The stem joint, sometimes swollen, at which leaves may rise.
Opposite.	With two leaves at a node; paired.
Ovule.	The female structure in the pistil that after fertilization becomes a seed.
Palmate.	In a spreading pattern like fingers on a hand. Refers to leaf venation and lobing.
Panicle.	A loose inflorescence, like the spikelets of grasses.
Parallel.	Referring to leaf venation; veins running side by side the length of the leaf blade, as in a grass leaf.
Perennial.	A plant whose life cycle may span 3 years or more.
Perianth.	The outer, similar flower parts considered together; may be sepals or both sepals and petals.
Petal.	A segment of the corolla (see Corolla); may be separate or fused to other petals.
Pinnate.	A featherlike arrangement with side branches or divisions extending along a central, elongate axis.
Raceme.	An elongate inflorescence on which individual flowers are distinctly stalked; see also Spike.
Rank.	The arrangement of leaves on a stem or in a basal tuft; in a 2-ranked pattern the leaves are all on one plane.
Ray or ray flower.	In the Composite Family, the flattened or straplike flowers on the edge of a head; often petallike.

41

Regular.	As applied to a flower, one that is radially symmetrical in shape. Perianth parts are all similar in size, shape, and arrangement. Includes wheel-, cup-, vase-, and tube-shaped flowers.
Rhizome.	See Rootstalk.
Rootstalk.	An underground stem, often growing parallel to the ground surface.
Rosette.	A spreading, flat-lying cluster of basal leaves.
Sepal.	A segment of the calyx (see Calyx); often green but may be colored; frequently small or falling early.
Spadix.	A dense, often fleshy, spike characteristic of the Arum Family; on it small flowers are crowded.
Spathe.	A leaflike or funnellike structure enclosing or associated with a spadix.
Spike.	An elongate inflorescence bearing flowers or flower heads that are essentially stalkless.
Spikelet.	A scaly or chaffy inflorescence, such as in grasses; a small spike.
Spur.	A saclike or tubelike flower structure, often part of a petal or sepal and containing nectar.
Stamen.	A slender, male flower structure bearing pollen; the third series of flower parts from the bottom or outside of the flower.
Stipule.	A leaflike structure borne in pairs at the base of the leaf stalk of some kinds of plants; may be free or fused and collarlike.
Taproot.	A root, usually unbranched and growing downward; like a carrot.
Tendril.	A slender, twining structure of a climbing plant; usually a modified leaf or leaflet.
Tuber.	The enlarged end of an underground stem, usually rounded and fleshy, in which food is stored.
Umbel.	A cluster of stalked flowers, all of which rise at about the same place like spokes in an umbrella.
Whorl.	A cluster of 3 or more leaves growing at the same stem node.

The Northland Wild Flowers: Descriptions and Portraits

List of Plant Families

(Common names are given in the text and index)

Descriptions and Portraits

Crowfoot Family

HEPATICA (*Hepatica*)

1. Sharp-lobed Hepatica (*H. acutiloba*). Also called Liverleaf. Woodland wild flower of early spring. The flowers have 5 to 12 (often 6) colored sepals ranging from white through pink, blue, and lavender. They stand on slender, hairy stems on which are 3 green, protective bracts. Later a clump of leaves develops. They are often mottled with purple or brown and have 3 pointed lobes. Occurrence: Minnesota — upland woods, mostly south and central; general — temperate eastern North America on limy soils.

The **Round-lobed Hepatica** (*H. americana*) has similar flowers, but the leaves have blunt or rounded lobes. It prefers acid soil and in Minnesota grows mostly in the north and east.

The name refers to the fancied resemblance of the leaf to a liver. The plant was once used to treat liver ailments.

1. Sharp-lobed Hepatica. Early spring.

45

2. Pasque Flower. Early spring.

Crowfoot Family

WINDFLOWER (*Anemone*)

2. Pasque Flower (*A. patens*). Also called Crocus. Early spring wild flower of prairies. The flower is about 2 inches across and has 5 to 7 pale purple sepals. It tops a hairy stem on which is a cluster (whorl) of divided, protective leaves. Usually there are several flowering stems in a clump. Within the flower is a ring of golden stamens and a central tuft of grayish pistils that become plumed fruits. In summer there is a clump of divided basal leaves. The plant is unpalatable to grazing animals. Occurrence: Minnesota — dry prairies and open hillsides in the south and west; general — much of western North America. Also in Eurasia.

Pasque Flower often blooms during the Easter (Paschal) season. To prairie children the hairy plants with bent flower buds were "Goslings." It is the floral emblem of South Dakota and Manitoba.

Crowfoot Family

3. Wood Anemone (*A. quinquefolia*). Also called Mayflower. A common spring wild flower of woods. The slender stem, usually less than 6 inches tall, is topped by a whorl of divided leaves above which is a single flower. The flower usually has 5 white, pink, or purplish sepals. Solitary divided leaves also rise from the elongate rootstalk. The plants often grow in patches. Occurrence: Minnesota — throughout much of the state but more common in the south and east; general — temperate eastern North America.

Anemone is an ancient name, possibly derived from the Greek word for wind, referring to open, windy places where some kinds of plants grow.

Crowfoot Family

4. Canada Anemone (*A. canadensis*). Also called Canada Windflower. Robust perennial, usually 1 to 2 feet tall, of moist, open places. It often grows in patches. The plant has deeply lobed basal leaves and an upright stem bearing a cluster (whorl) of cut leaves from which the long-stalked,

46

3. Wood Anemone. Spring.

white flowers rise. They are 1 to 1½ inches across and have 5, sometimes 4, petallike sepals. Occurrence: Minnesota — throughout, often along roads and railways; general — much of temperate North America but not in the far west.

Worldwide there are about 85 species of *Anemone*, some of which are raised for the beauty of their flowers. All have a whorl of leaves on the stem above which the flowers rise.

4. Canada Anemone. Spring; early summer.

47

5. Long-fruited Thimbleweed. Summer.

5. Long-fruited Thimbleweed (*A. cylindrica*). Plant of dry, open places. It has clumped basal leaves and an upright stem with a whorl of 3 or more deeply lobed and cut leaves. The long-stalked, dish-shaped flowers are about 1 inch across and have 5 greenish white sepals. Fruits (achenes) are in an elongate cluster, 2 to 5 times longer than wide, that resembles the rough part of a thimble. When mature, the achenes are covered with matted, cottony hairs. Occurrence: Minnesota — throughout; general — temperate North America.

The **Virginia Thimbleweed** (*A. virginiana*) is similar but has a shorter "thimble" about twice as long as wide. It is mostly a plant of open woods and clearings.

Crowfoot Family

RUE ANEMONE (*Anemonella*)

6. Rue Anemone (*A. thalictroides*). This graceful, spring wild flower is quite similar to the true anemones. The slender stems, often clumped, rise from a tuft of compound basal leaves, each with 9 leaflets. Near the top of the stem is a whorl of leaflets and several slender-stalked flowers with 4 to 10 white or pink sepals. The fruits, as in *Anemone*, are achenes. Elongate tubers are produced at the base of the upright stems. Occurrence: Minnesota — rich, upland forests and clearings, mostly in the southeastern third; general — eastern U.S.

There is a cultivar with double flowers.

Crowfoot Family

FALSE RUE ANEMONE
(*Isopyrum*)

7. False Rue Anemone (*I. biternatum*). Superficially much like Rue Anemone but different in several respects. The white flowers rise in the axils of scattered stem leaves and not above a whorl of leaflets. The fruit is a pod (follicle) containing seeds, and the roots are fibrous with small tubers along them. A common and beautiful, spring wild flower of moist woods and floodplain forests where it often grows in patches covering the forest floor. Occurrence: Minnesota — southeastern third; general — eastern U.S. and adjacent Canada.

6. Rue Anemone. Spring.

7. False Rue Anemone. Spring.

8. Marsh Marigold. Early spring.

Crowfoot Family

MARSH MARIGOLD (*Caltha*)

8. Marsh Marigold (*C. palustris*). Also called Cowslip. In the spring, marshes, especially along streams, may be bright with its golden yellow blossoms. The "chaliced" flowers,

9. Early Buttercup. Early spring.

as Shakespeare called them, are clustered and 1 to 2 inches across. Each has 5 to 7 (often 6) showy sepals and many yellow stamens. Leaves are broadly heart-shaped or rounded and usually coarsely toothed. *Caltha* is derived from the Latin word for cup, and marigold probably comes from Anglo-Saxon, meaning "marsh-gold." Cattle and deer avoid eating this plant. Occurrence: Minnesota — throughout except in the southwest; general — circumboreal, in North America from arctic south to temperate U.S.

Crowfoot Family

BUTTERCUP (*Ranunculus*)

9. Early Buttercup (*R. fascicularis*). Early spring wild flower of open woods, prairies, and sunny hillsides. Usually less than 10 inches tall, it has spreading stems and divided leaves covered with silky hairs. The flowers are about ¾ inch across with 5 pale yellow petals and 5 small, green sepals. Occurrence: Minnesota — mostly in the southeast; general — temperate eastern North America. The **Prairie Buttercup** (*R. rhom-*

50

boideus) also blossoms early. The lower leaves are undivided and toothed, and the flowering stem is branched. In Minnesota it is found mostly on prairies in the south and west.

Crowfoot Family

10. Tall Buttercup (*R. acris*). A conspicuous buttercup of brushy places, pastures, fields, and roadsides. The bright yellow flowers, up to 1 inch across, are on erect, branching stems, often 2 feet tall. Blossoms in early summer. Leaves are deeply lobed and cut in a palmate or "crowfoot" pattern. The acrid juice makes it unpalatable to cattle. Occurrence: Minnesota — most common in the northeastern third; general — a European species widely naturalized in North America.

Crowfoot Family

11. Swamp Buttercup (*R. septentrionalis*). Buttercup of moist woods, swamps, and floodplains. Flowers are bright yellow and about an inch across. In early spring the stem is short and erect, but later it elongates and spreads and arches. The leaves are compound with 3 stalked leaflets. Occurrence: Minnesota — throughout; general — temperate eastern North America.

The **Yellow Water Crowfoot** (*R. flabellaris*) also has yellow flowers about an inch across. They are on hollow stems that stand above the shallow water of ponds in springtime. The leaves are submersed and cut into many thin, ribbonlike segments. This species was once abundant in prairie ponds and wetlands that have been drained and are now fields of corn and soybeans.

51

10. Tall Buttercup. Late Spring; summer.

11. Swamp Buttercup. Spring; summer.

12. Virgin's Bower. Summer.

Crowfoot Family

VIRGIN'S BOWER (*Clematis*)

12. Virgin's Bower (*C. virginiana*). Also called Old Man's Beard. Sprawling or climbing vine with square stems and opposite, compound leaves with 3 leaflets. Leaf stalks twist around other objects. The small flowers are clustered and have 4 creamy-white sepals. Later the flowers develop into beardlike tufts of plumed achenes. This ornamental perennial vine is easily grown on a trellis or can be used as a trailing ground cover. Occurrence: Minnesota — throughout in open or semishady places; general — temperate eastern North America.

The **Purple Virgin's Bower** (*C. verticillaris*) has large blue flowers much like those of a garden clematis. In Minnesota it grows in rocky, wooded, and brushy places, mostly in the east and northeast.

Crowfoot Family

LARKSPUR (*Delphinium*)

13. Prairie Larkspur (*D. virescens*). Perennial of dry prairies and open hillsides. The stems, usually 1 to 3 feet tall, end in a spikelike cluster of white flowers. Each flower has 5 sepals, the uppermost ending in a spur, and 4 crowded, irregular petals in the center. Both basal and stem leaves are much cut and divided. New growth is toxic to cattle. Occurrence: Minnesota — south and west; general — prairies and plains of central and western North America.

Delphinium stems from the Latin word for dolphin and refers to the fancied resemblance of the spurred flower to this aquatic mammal.

13. Prairie Larkspur. Late spring; summer.

14. Columbine. Spring.

Crowfoot Family

COLUMBINE (*Aquilegia*)

14. Columbine (*A. canadensis*). Also called Honeysuckle. A graceful, usually clumped, wild flower of open woods and brushy and rocky places. It commonly grows 1 to 3 feet tall and has compound basal and stem leaves. The nodding flower has 5 scarlet sepals ending in long spurs, and between them 5 spreading yellow petals. Shiny, black seeds are produced in a cluster of erect pods. Occurrence: Minnesota — throughout; general — temperate eastern and central North America.

Columbine refers to the resemblance of the flowers to a flock of doves and *Aquilegia* likens the spurs to claws of eagles. Both avian analogies are more applicable to the short-spurred, European columbine than to ours.

53

15. Tall Meadow Rue. Late spring; summer.

16. Early Meadow Rue. Spring.

MEADOW RUE (*Thalictrum*)

15. Tall Meadow Rue (*T. dasycarpum*). A wind-pollinated member of the Crowfoot Family. It has plumes of small flowers in which the showy parts are the dangling white or yellow stamens (on plants with male flowers) or the purplish clusters of pistils (on plants with female flowers). This clumped perennial of moist meadows and brushy places is often taller than 3 feet. Leaflets of the compound leaves are longer than wide and end in 3 pointed lobes. Occurrence: Minnesota — throughout; general — much of temperate North America.

Crowfoot Family

16. Early Meadow Rue (*T. dioicum*) is similar to the preceding species but less robust. It commonly grows in moist woods as clumps 1 to 2 feet tall. Leaflets are about as wide as long and end in 3 blunt lobes. Found throughout Minnesota and temperate eastern North America.

The **Veiny Meadow Rue** (*T. venulosum*) of prairies and open places with coarse soil is similar but has leaflets with a rough pattern of veins beneath and scattered stems rising from running rootstalks.

Crowfoot Family

BANEBERRY (*Actaea*)

17. Red Baneberry (*A. rubra*). Perennial of woods. It is usually 1 to 2 feet tall with a clumped, bushy appearance and has compound leaves with many sharply toothed leaflets. In spring the plant bears a fluffy cluster of small, white flowers and in summer shiny red, or sometimes white, berries. Each berry is on a slender stalk. Occurrence: Minnesota — throughout; general — temperate North America.

The similar **White Baneberry** (*A. pachypoda*), also called Doll's Eyes, is more robust and has berries that are usually white with a dark spot, "the pupil." The berries stand out from the stem on thick, reddish stalks. In Minnesota White Baneberry is most common in the southeast. Berries and roots of both species are poisonous.

17. Red Baneberry. Spring.

17a. Red Baneberry in fruit. Summer.

18. Blue Cohosh. Spring.   18a. Blue Cohosh in fruit. Summer.

Barberry Family

BLUE COHOSH (*Caulophyllum*)

18. Blue Cohosh (*C. thalictroides*). Perennial of moist woods. When mature it has a spreading, somewhat bushy appearance and is often 2 to 3 feet tall. The compound leaves have wide, thick leaflets that end in 3 or 5 blunt lobes. In spring when in flower the developing stems and leaves are often purplish and the clustered flowers have 6 yellow or purplish sepals. Later globular, blue berries develop, each on a thick stalk. Occurrence: Minnesota — throughout, except in the northeast, mostly in hardwood forests; general — temperate North America. Also in eastern Asia.

The roots, which contain glucosides, once had medicinal uses. The word *Cohosh* is of Algonkian Indian origin and means "rough."

Water Lily Family

YELLOW WATER LILY (*Nuphar*)

19. Yellow Water Lily (*N. variegatum*). Also called Pond Lily. A common aquatic plant of lakeshores and slow stretches of streams. The floating heart-shaped leaves and yellow flowers rise from a thick rootstalk on the bottom. Flowers are cup-shaped, about 2 inches across, and have 5 or 6 deep yellow sepals that are often reddish at the base. There are many small, fleshy petals and many stamens. The pistil matures beneath the water and becomes a pod filled with large, spherical seeds. These are eaten by ducks. Occurrence: Minnesota — throughout; general — much of northern U.S. and adjacent Canada.

The leaves and rootstalks are food for moose and beavers.

19. Yellow Water Lily. Summer.

20. White Water Lily. Summer.

Water Lily Family

WHITE WATER LILY (*Nymphaea*)

20. White Water Lily (*N. tuberosa*). Common in shallow water, especially along lakeshores where the bottom is mucky. The floating leaves are circular, deeply notched at the base, and green beneath. The double white flower is about 6 inches across and has petals that merge with the stamens, forming a continuous, transitional series. Short branches of the rootstalks sometimes break off and form new plants. Occurrence: Minnesota — throughout; general — eastern U.S. and adjacent Canada.

The similar **Sweet-scented White Water Lily** (*N. odorata*) has leaves that are purplish beneath and sweet-scented flowers sometimes tinged with pink. In Minnesota it is most common in the north.

57

21. American Lotus Lily. Summer.

Water Lily Family

LOTUS LILY (*Nelumbo*)

21. American Lotus Lily (*N. lutea*). Commonly called Lotus. Our largest wild flower, the pale yellow blossoms being 6 to 10 inches across when fully open. It grows in shallow water and in marshes subject to flooding. The circular leaf blade, as wide as 2 feet, has a central stalk and at first floats on the water surface. Later both blossoms and stem rise several feet above the surface of the water. The top-shaped pod has large seeds in depressions in the up-

per surface. This species is closely related to the pink Sacred Lotus of Asia. Occurrence: Minnesota — shallow lakes and marshes along the Mississippi River between St. Paul and Iowa. It is also found in a few lakes in the vicinity of the Twin Cities, where it may have been planted by Indians who used both the seeds and the starchy rootstalks for food; general — eastern U.S.

Poppy Family

BLOODROOT (*Sanguinaria*)

22. Bloodroot (*S. canadensis*). An early spring wild flower of moist rich woods. The elongate buds, which are first protected by 2 green sepals and sheathed in a rolled-up leaf, open as pristine white flowers. They have 8 or 12 petals and a golden tuft of stamens. The petals soon drop and an elongate seed pod develops. Leaves are basal, stalked, and have wide, irregularly lobed blades. All parts of the plant have orange-red juice which was used by the Indians for war paint and dye. Occurrence: Minnesota — throughout, except in the extreme west and northeast; general — east, temperate North America.

22. Bloodroot. Spring.

Fumitory Family

CORYDALIS (*Corydalis*)

23. Golden Corydalis (*C. aurea*). A low plant of open woods and clearings, often in sandy or rocky places. The clustered golden-yellow flowers are irregularly shaped with one of the 4 petals ending in a blunt spur. Leaves are much divided and the stem often branched and spreading. Seeds are produced in curved pods. Occurrence: Minnesota — throughout, except in the southwest; general — north-central and western U.S. and adjacent Canada.

Pale Corydalis (*C. sempervirens*) has similar irregular flowers but they are pink, tipped with yellow. Often it has sprawling stems. It grows in woods and rocky or brushy places, mostly in the north.

Corydalis is Greek for *horned lark*.

23. Golden Corydalis. Spring; summer.

24. Dutchman's Breeches. Spring.

Fumitory Family

DUTCHMAN'S BREECHES
(*Dicentra*)

24. Dutchman's Breeches (*D. cucullaria*). Low perennial of rich woods. It has much-divided leaves in a basal clump and slender, often arching, stems along which are the nodding, white, or sometimes pink, flowers. They have 4 petals, 2 extending backward as blunt, spreading spurs — the "legs" of the "breeches." They contain nectar that can be reached by long-tongued moths or by bees strong enough to push apart the petals. The small, clustered tubers contain alkaloids and were once used medicinally. Cows have been poisoned by eating them. Occurrence: Minnesota — widely distributed, but most common in the southeast; general — temperate eastern North America.

59

Mustard Family

WINTER CRESS (*Barbarea*)

25. Winter Cress (*B. vulgaris*). A biennial mustard that flowers in spring. The plants, usually 2 to 3 feet tall, stand out as bright yellow clumps in moist meadows and fields. The small, 4-petaled flowers are in elongate clusters, and the leaves and stems are hairless. Lower leaves are deeply lobed, with the end lobe the largest. Occurrence: A European plant that is widely naturalized in Minnesota and elsewhere in North America.

In medieval times Winter Cress was used as a poultice on wounds and was appropriately dedicated to St. Barbara, the patron saint of artillerymen.

25. Winter Cress. Spring.

26. Toothwort. Spring.

Mustard Family

TOOTHWORT (*Dentaria*)

26. Toothwort (*D. laciniata*). A spring wild flower which often grows in patches in moist woods. The stem, usually less than a foot tall, ends in a cluster of 4-petaled pink or white flowers, each about ½ inch across. They stand above a whorl of stem leaves that are deeply lobed and coarsely toothed. Both the common and generic names refer to segments of the rootstalk that somewhat resemble teeth. Occurrence: Minnesota — mostly in the southeastern third but occasionally northward to St. Louis County; general — temperate eastern North America.

Mustard Family

SPRING CRESS (*Cardamine*)

27. Spring Cress (*C. bulbosa*). A low

60

27. Spring Cress. Spring.

perennial, usually less than a foot tall, of marshes, wet meadows, and spring areas. The white, 4-petaled flowers are in a fairly compact cluster, and the stems are smooth and leafy. Blades of lower leaves are rounded. Small tubers develop at the base of the stem. Occurrence: Minnesota — throughout, except in the northeast; general — much of temperate eastern North America.

Other common, white-flowered mustards include **Water Cress** (*Nasturtium officinale*), the brittle-stemmed salad plant of limy streams and springy areas, and **Hoary Alyssum** (*Berteroa incana*), a weedy annual of dry, open places. The latter is gray with stiff hairs and has globular pods.

Mustard Family

SWEET ROCKET (*Hesperis*)

28. Sweet Rocket (*H. matronalis*). Also called Dame's Violet. Robust biennial, usually 3 to 4 feet tall, that has long been grown in gardens and often escapes to shady spots along roads. The flowers are usually deep purple but may be white or

shades between. They have 4 petals, are about an inch across, and are markedly sweet-scented in the evening. The herbage is covered with soft hairs. Occurrence: a native of Europe widely established throughout eastern North America.

28. Sweet Rocket. Spring.

61

Pitcher Plant Family

PITCHER PLANT (*Sarracenia*)

29. Pitcher Plant (*S. purpurea*). Insectiverous plant of bogs and wet, sedgy swamps. It has a rosette of pitcher-shaped leaves. These partly fill with water. Insects find descent into the pitcher easy, but downward pointing hairs hinder climbing out. Drowned insects are broken down by enzymes and bacteria, and provide nutrients for the plant. The dark red flowers, about 2 inches across, are nodding and single on leafless stems. Occurrence: Minnesota — mostly in the north; general — subarctic North America south to southeastern U.S.

29. Pitcher Plant. Summer.

30. Bishop's Cap. Spring; summer.

Saxifrage Family

BISHOP'S CAP (*Mitella*)

30. Bishop's Cap (*M. diphylla*). Also called Miterwort. A low, graceful perennial of moist woods. It has basal leaves with heart-shaped blades that are lobed and toothed. The slender stem bears a pair of small leaves and ends in an elongate inflorescence of small, white flowers. Each flower has 5 sepals and 5 fringed petals. Occurrence: Minnesota — mostly in the southeast and south; general — temperate eastern North America.

Northern Bishop's Cap (*M. nuda*) has similar flowers but they are on a leafless stem. Leaves are all basal with rounded, shallowly lobed blades. The upper leaf surface has short, upright hairs. A wide-ranging species of northern wet woods and bogs.

The name refers to the shape of the pod.

62

31. Alum Root. Summer.

Saxifrage Family

ALUM ROOT (*Heuchera*)

31. Alum Root (*H. richardsonii*). Plant of dry prairies and open woods. The stem, usually 1 to 2 feet tall, ends in an elongate cluster of irregularly shaped green or brownish flowers. There is a clump of basal leaves with rounded or heart-shaped blades that are lobed and on hairy stalks. Occurrence: Minnesota — throughout; general — upper Midwest and Great Plains.

The thick, astringent root was used medicinally by Indians.

Saxifrage Family

GRASS OF PARNASSUS
(*Parnassia*)

32. Northern Grass of Parnassus (*P. palustris*). Low plant of shores and marshes. Characterized by a basal clump of rounded somewhat heart-shaped leaves. The slender stem bears a single, small leaf and ends in a solitary, white flower which has 5 spreading petals. Occurrence: Minnesota — mostly in the central and north; general — circumpolar, in North America from arctic south to northern U.S.

The similar **Thick-leaved Grass of Parnassus** (*P. glauca*) has bluish-green leaf blades that are rounded or somewhat tapering at the base. In Minnesota it is found mostly in wet places along the prairie edges from the southeast to northwest.

Rose Family

WILD ROSE (*Rosa*)

33. Prairie Wild Rose (*R. arkansana*). Low wild rose of prairies. Usually less than 1½ feet tall, the erect woody stems are very prickly and topped with a cluster of pink or rosy flowers. Ripe fruits or "hips" are bright red, often somewhat flattened, and retain the sepals. Occurrence: Minnesota — open places, mostly in the south and west; general — central North America. It is the state flower of North Dakota.

The **Smooth Wild Rose** (*R. blanda*) grows to 3 feet high, and has few or no prickles on the upper main stem and side branches. The flowers open in small clusters. Widespread and common in open and brushy areas.

32. Northern Grass of Parnassus. Summer.

33. Prairie Wild Rose. Summer.

34. Prickly Wild Rose. Summer.

Rose Family

34. Prickly Wild Rose (*R. acicularis*). Robust wild rose of wooded country. The prickly, often arching, stems may be taller than 6 feet. Flowers mostly open singly and are scattered over the bush. Occurrence: Minnesota — common in the north along roads and in forest openings; general — northern temperate North America. Also in Siberia.

Wild rose hips were eaten by Indians but only as a starvation diet. They are now known to be high in vitamin C. The flowers provide pollen but no nectar for bees.

65

35. Marsh Cinquefoil. Summer.

36. Shrubby Cinquefoil. Summer.

Rose Family

CINQUEFOIL (*Potentilla*)

35. Marsh Cinquefoil (*P. palustris*). Erect reddish plant of marshes and bogs, sometimes with the lower parts growing in water. The stem, 1 to 3 feet tall, ends in a loose cluster of reddish-purple flowers and has pinnately compound leaves. Occurrence: Minnesota — most common in the north; general — circumpolar subarctic, ranging south in North America to northern U.S.

Rose Family

36. Shrubby Cinquefoil (*P. fruticosa*). Low, much branched, and often bushy shrub, up to 3 feet tall. The tough woody stems have shredded bark and bear bright yellow flowers and small pinnately compound leaves. Occurrence: Minnesota — mostly in the north. Common on rocky headlands along Lake Superior; general — circumpolar subarctic south in North America to northern U.S. It is found in habitats ranging from marshes to well-drained, open and brushy uplands.

Shrubby Cinquefoil resists browsing, and we have seen it flourishing on heavily grazed bison ranges in parks in South Dakota and Manitoba. When grown in gardens it is called Gold Drops.

Rose Family

37. Tall Cinquefoil (*P. arguta*). Erect perennial, 1 to 3 feet tall, of dry prairies, fields, and open woods. Stems are usually clumped and have pinnately compound leaves covered with soft, white hairs. Flowers are pale yellow to almost white. Occurrence: Minnesota — throughout; general – subarctic North America south to central U.S.

The **Sulfur Cinquefoil** (*P. recta*) is also an upright plant of dry fields and prairies. It has spreading clusters of deep yellow flowers, about 1 inch across. Leaves are palmately compound with 5 to 7 coarsely toothed leaflets. This European plant is widely naturalized in eastern U.S.

Rose Family

38. Old Field Cinquefoil (*P. simplex*). Plant with slender, leafy stems that eventually elongate, become arching or trailing, and root at the ends. The palmately compound leaves have 5 leaflets. Flowers are at the end of slender stalks. Occurence: Minnesota — fields, open woods, and roadsides, mostly in the south and east; general — eastern U.S. and adjacent Canada.

37. Tall Cinquefoil. Summer.

38. Old Field Cinquefoil. Summer.

39. Three-toothed Cinquefoil. Summer.

Rose Family

39. Three-toothed Cinquefoil (*P. tridentata*). Low plant, usually less than 6 inches tall, with a woody base. It has compound leaves with 3 thick leaflets, each ending in 3 coarse teeth. Its small, white flowers are in a spreading cluster. Occur-

rence: Minnesota — dry, open places, often on sand or rocks. Common on cliffs along Lake Superior; general — subarctic North America south to eastern U.S.

This cinquefoil is sometimes planted as an interesting and hardy ground cover.

40. Yellow Avens. Summer.

41. Purple Avens. Spring, summer.

Rose Family

AVENS (*Geum*)

40. Yellow Avens (*G. alleppicum* var. *strictum*). Perennial of moist, open or brushy places. The erect stem, usually 2 to 4 feet tall, has pinnately compound leaves with leaflets that vary considerably in shape and size. The yellow flowers, 1 to 2 inches across, have 5 petals and a cluster of long pistils in the center. These later become a spiny head of dry fruits. Occurrence: Minnesota — throughout; general — temperate North America.

Rose Family

41. Purple Avens (*G. triflorum*). Also called Prairie Smoke. This low, reddish plant of prairies is usually less than 1 foot tall and grows in clumps or patches. The elongate leaves are pinnately compound, with many leaflets that are toothed and covered with soft hairs. The nodding flowers have conspicuous, purple sepals. After flowering, the styles elongate to form an erect brush of soft, slender plumes, the "Prairie Smoke." Occurrence: Minnesota — prairies, mostly in the south and west; general — temperate central and western North America.

42. Flowering Raspberry. Summer.

Rose Family

42. Flowering Raspberry (*R. parviflorus*). Also called Thimbleberry. One of the most conspicuous, early summer wild flowers along roads near Lake Superior. The unarmed,

43. Partridge Pea. Summer.

woody, and herbaceous stems are commonly 2 to 4 feet tall, and have wide, lobed leaves, somewhat like maple leaves. The showy, white flowers, about 2 inches across, have 5 spreading petals and many stamens. The stamens are pale when the flower first appears, but they darken with age. The flat, orange-red raspberries that follow have a rather bland flavor but make tasty jam. Occurrence: Minnesota — mostly in the northeast; general — from Ontario westward to northwestern North America. It is abundant on Isle Royale in Lake Superior.

Bean Family

PARTRIDGE PEA (*Cassia*)

43. Partridge Pea (*C. fasciculata*). Also called Sensitive Pea. Annual with erect stems, usually 1 to 2 feet tall. Leaves are pinnately compound with 20 to 30 leaflets, always an even number. It has yellow flowers with 5 petals of several sizes. They are followed by elongate, hairy pods. The leaves are remarkably sensitive. Leaflets fold when disturbed or when the plant is under stress in

70

hot, dry weather. Occurrence: Minnesota — mostly in the southeast in sandy, open, or brushy places; general — eastern U.S.

Bean Family

LUPINE (*Lupinus*)

44. Wild Lupine (*L. perennis*). A handsome wild flower with elongate, spikelike clusters of blue flowers. It usually grows on sandy soil and is 1 to 3 feet tall. The leaves are palmately compound with 7 to 11 leaflets. The fruit is a hairy pod. Occurrence: Minnesota — sandy prairies and woods in the central and southeast; general — eastern U.S.

Its name is derived from *lupus*, the Latin word for "wolf," and is based on the ancient but mistaken assumption that since Lupine grows on poor soils it is responsible for this condition.

44. Wild Lupine. Late spring; summer.

45. Bird's-foot Trefoil. Summer.

45a. Bird's-foot Trefoil, along roadside. Summer.

Bean Family

BIRD'S-FOOT TREFOIL (*Lotus*)

45. Bird's-foot Trefoil (*L. corniculatus*). A European legume that is widely established and forms showy, yellow patches along highways where it is sometimes planted to control erosion. The pale green stems are sprawling and spreading. They bear leaves with 5 leaflets (the lower pair are really stipules) and rounded clusters of bright yellow flowers. Later "bird's feet" of erect, slender pods develop. Occurrence: Minnesota — throughout but most common in the north; general — temperate eastern North America and Pacific Coast.

Bean Family

CLOVER (*Trifolium*)

46. White Clover (*T. repens*). Low perennial of open, grassy places. The creeping stems and rootstalks bear compound leaves, each with 3 finely toothed leaflets and rounded heads of small, white flowers. Each head is on a slender, leafless stalk. It is probably the true Irish shamrock. Occurrence: A European species that has long been planted as a component of pastures and lawns, and which is widely naturalized on well-drained soils.

Alsike Clover (*T. hybridum*) is similar but has pink, markedly sweet-scented flowers on upright, leafy stems. It is also of European origin, coming from Alsike, Sweden. Frequently it has escaped from hayfields to roadsides.

46. White Clover. Late spring; summer.

47. Red Clover. Spring, summer.

Bean Family

47. Red Clover (*T. pratense*). A robust clover, usually 1 to 2 feet tall, with hairy stems and rounded heads of rosy-red flowers. There is often a dark spot on the leaflets of the compound leaves. The flowers are usually pollinated by bumblebees. Occurrence: this native of Eurasia is sometimes grown for forage and is widely naturalized in North America.

Rabbit's-foot Clover (*T. arvense*), also from Europe, is an annual with hairy stems and elongate, silky, gray heads of white or pink flowers. It grows on road shoulders and in sandy fields.

Bean Family

SWEET CLOVER (*Melilotus*)

48. Yellow Sweet Clover (*M. officinalis*). A common roadside plant, usually 2 to 4 feet tall, with small, yellow flowers in elongate, upright clusters. The plant is usually biennial and grows as a clump of several stems. Leaves are compound with 3 toothed leaflets. Occurrence: a European species sometimes grown for pasture and hay. Widely naturalized.

The **White Sweet Clover** (*M. alba*) is similar but has white flowers. It is also of European origin and widely naturalized. Both species are good nectar sources for honeybees. Sweet clover releases the vanillalike odor of coumarin when being dried for hay.

48. Yellow Sweet Clover. Summ

Bean Family

PSORALEA (*Psoralea*)

49. Silver-leaved Psoralea (*P. argophylla*). Also called Scurf Pea. A common prairie perennial with leaves and stems covered with soft, white hairs. Stems are branched, somewhat zigzag, and usually 1 to 2 feet tall. Leaves are palmately compound with 3 or 5 leaflets. It has small, blue flowers. Occurrence: Minnesota – dry prairies, mostly in the south and west; general – prairies and plains of upper central and western U.S. and adjacent Canada.

Bean Family

50. Prairie Turnip (*P. esculenta*). Also called Pomme Blanche and Indian Potato. An important food plant of plains Indians, who dug the thick, turnip-like root to obtain the central, starchy portion. The plant, which grows to a height of 18 inches, has an upright, hairy stem and palmately compound leaves with 5 elongate leaflets. The small, blue flowers are in a dense, oblong cluster. The Dakota Indians called it Teepsenee and early French explorers of Minnesota named the Pomme de Terre River after it. Occurrence: Minnesota – in the south and west on prairies, often where hilly; general – prairies and plains, north central and western U.S. and adjacent Canada.

49. Silver-leaved Psoralea. Summer.

50. Prairie Turnip. Summer.

Bean Family

LEAD PLANT (*Amorpha*)

51. Lead Plant (*A. canescens*). Perennial of prairies. The erect, somewhat woody, stems are usually 1 to 2 feet tall. They are tipped by taper-

76

51. Lead Plant. Summer.

ing spikes of small, blue flowers, each having a single petal that is shorter than the golden-yellow stamens. Leaves are pinnately compound with many leaflets. They are gray with soft hairs, giving the plant both its leaden hue and its name. Occurrence: Minnesota — prairies; general — temperate western North America.

Because its tough rootstalks hindered plowing, pioneer prairie farmers called it "Devil's Shoestrings." To Ponca Indians it was "Buffalo-bellow Plant" because it blossomed when bison were in rut.

Bean Family

PRAIRIE CLOVER
(*Petalostemum*)

52. Purple Prairie Clover (*P. purpureum*). A common perennial of dry prairies. The slender, erect stems, usually about 2 feet tall, are topped by elongate heads of purple flowers. It often grows in patches. Leaves are pinnately compound with narrow leaflets that are dotted beneath. Occurrence: Minnesota — dry prairies and open places but uncommon in

the northeast; general — temperate central and western North America.

The **White Prairie Clover** (*P. candidum*) is similar in appearance and distribution but has white flowers and is usually somewhat taller than Purple Prairie Clover.

52. Purple Prairie Clover. Summer.

77

53. Canada Milk Vetch. Summer.

Bean Family

MILK VETCH (*Astragalus*)

53. Canada Milk Vetch (*A. canadensis*). Robust, often clumped perennial with erect stems 1 to 4 feet tall. It has pinnately compound leaves with many leaflets and elongate, rather loose clusters of white or yellowish flowers. These are followed by short, ascending pods. Occurrence: Minnesota — throughout on moist prairies, along streams, and in open woods; general — much of temperate U.S. and adjacent Canada.

Bean Family

54. Prairie Plum (*A. crassicarpus*). Low, clumped perennial, usually with several spreading stems and seldom taller than 1 foot. It has pinnately compound leaves with many small leaflets and rounded

54. Prairie Plum. Spring.

clusters of purple or sometimes whitish flowers about an inch long. The thick-walled, inflated pods commonly lie on the ground. They are shaped like small plums and when young have a texture and flavor much like garden peas. Occurrence: Minnesota — dry prairies in the south and west, often on hills and bluffs; general — prairies and plains of western U.S. and adjacent Canada.

Bean Family

LOCOWEED (*Oxytropis*)

55. Locoweed (*O. lambertii*). Low perennial of prairies. It has a basal clump of pinnately compound leaves that tend to stand upright. They are covered with silky hairs. Flowers are reddish-purple and in an elongate cluster on a leafless stalk. The keel of the flower has a point at the front end (tip), in this respect differing from several more western locoweeds of the genus *Astragalus*. Occurrence: Minnesota — dry prairies, mostly in the west, but uncommon. It was once common on the hills along the upper Minnesota River; general — Great Plains.

Locoweed has long been known to be poisonous to stock. Animals become addicted to it, lose muscular coordination, and become lethargic — "go loco."

55. Locoweed. Summer.

56. Crown Vetch. Summer.

57. Pointed-leaved Tick Trefoil. Summer.

CROWN VETCH (*Coronilla*)

56. Crown Vetch (*C. varia*). Perennial with spreading, sprawling stems, pinnately compound leaves, and pink and white flowers in rounded crownlike clusters. It is planted to control soil erosion along highways. In early summer roadside bank cuts may be pink with the numerous flowers. Occurrence: a native of Europe, Asia, and North Africa. It is widely established in eastern North America and often crowds out native plants.

Bean Family

TICK TREFOIL (*Desmodium*)

57. Pointed-leaved Tick Trefoil (*D. glutinosum*). Summer wild flower of woods and woodland edges. Usually 2 to 3 feet tall, the upright stem bears a cluster of large, compound leaves, each with 3 leaflets. Above these are slender, flowering stalks with many pink or purplish flowers. Flowers are followed by flat, jointed pods covered with tiny, hooked hairs. The pods break into segments when mature and adhere to clothing and fur. Occurrence: Minnesota — mostly in the southern half in hardwood forests; general — temperate eastern North America.

Bean Family

58. Canada Tick Trefoil (*D. canadense*). Robust, erect, and often clumped perennial of dry, open, and brushy places. Usually 3 to 4 feet tall. The purple flowers are in elongate clusters that are branched and somewhat leafy. Stems and compound leaves are hairy. Pods are similar to those of the preceding species. Occurrence: Minnesota — throughout except in the northeast; general — temperate eastern North America.

Bean Family

VETCH (*Vicia*)

59. Tufted Vetch (*V. cracca*). Also called Bird Vetch. Climbing or sprawling vine, commonly 2 to 3 feet long, with 1-sided clusters of many (9 to 30) blue or purple flowers and pinnately compound leaves ending in a tendril. Hairs on the stem lie flat and are inconspicuous. The **Hairy Vetch** (*V. villosa*) is similar but has soft, spreading hairs. Occurrence: Both species are of European origin but are widely naturalized in Minnesota and elsewhere in North America.

The **American Vetch** (*V. americana*) is a widely distributed vine of open woods and brushy places. It has purple flowers in clusters of 2 to 9. The paired stipules (leaflike stuctures at the base of the compound leaves) are sharply toothed.

58. Canada Tick Trefoil. Summer.

59. Tufted Vetch. Spring summer.

81

60. Purple Pea. Spring, summer.

Bean Family

WILD PEA (*Lathyrus*)

60. Purple Pea (*L. venosus*). Vine rising from a rootstalk. Flowers are purple or bicolored purple and white and in an elongate cluster of 10 or more. Leaves are compound, end in a tendril, and have stipules (paired leaflike structures at the base of the leafstalk) that are smaller than the leaflets. Occurrence: Minnesota — throughout in woods and brushy. places and on prairies; general — temperate North America.

The **Pale Vetchling** (*L. ochroleucus*), also called White Pea, has yellowish-white flowers, pale foliage, and stipules larger than the side leaflets. It occurs mostly in woods and brushy places.

Bean Family

61. Beach Pea (*L. japonicus*). Quite similar to the Purple Pea but usually lower growing and with stipules larger than the side leaflets. Occurrence: circumpolar on beaches of oceans and large northern lakes. In Minnesota it is common on beaches of Lake Superior. It is doubtful that the seeds of this and other wild peas are edible, although in Europe Beach Pea has been used for food in times of famine.

The **Marsh Pea** (*L. palustris*) grows in marshes and along shores. It has purple flowers, leaves with stipules much smaller than the narrow leaflets, and often winged (flanged) stems. It is found throughout much of Minnesota.

Bean Family

GROUNDNUT (*Apios*)

62. Groundnut (*A. americana*). Twining vine of moist woods, thickets, and stream banks. Leaves are compound, usually with 3 or 5 leaf-

61. Beach Pea. Summer.

62. Groundnut. Summer.

lets. The fragrant, brown-purple flowers are in rounded clusters. Along the rootstalks are small tubers that were once used for food by Indians. It is likely that the plant is spread along streams by tubers washed away during floods. Occurrence: Minnesota — mostly in the south; general — temperate eastern North America.

The tubers were eaten by the Pilgrims during their first winter in New England. Groundnut was early taken to Europe as a prospective crop plant. It was found, however, that several years were required to produce a sizable crop of tubers.

63. Hog Peanut. Summer.

64. Violet Wood Sorrel. Spring; summer.

Bean Family

HOG PEANUT (*Amphicarpa*)

63. Hog Peanut (*A. bracteata*). Slender, twining vine of moist woods, thickets, and banks. Leaves are compound with 3 broad leaflets. On the upper part of the vine there are small, white to purple flowers in loose clusters. Near the base are other flowers that are nearly or entirely without petals. They are directed downward and produce rounded 1-seeded pods, often underground. These are the "hog peanuts." Occurrence: Minnesota — throughout except in the southwest; general — eastern temperate North America.

Oxalis Family

WOOD SORREL (*Oxalis*)

64. Violet Wood Sorrel (*O. violacea*). Low plant, a few inches tall,

84

with a clump of basal leaves. The small leaf is compound with 3 leaflets, each notched at the end. Flowers are violet and in a small cluster at the end of the stalk. They have 5 spreading petals. Occurrence: Minnesota — woods and prairies, mostly in the south; general — eastern U.S.

Leaves of this and the following species of *Oxalis* contain oxalic acid and have a sour taste. Both sorrel and *oxalis* mean "sour." Children often call the plant Sauerkraut or Sour Grass.

mon, sometimes weedy plant of open and shady places, especially where the soil has been disturbed. The leaves are like those of the preceding species, but the plant has a slender rootstalk by which it spreads. Flowers are yellow in a loose cluster. Occurrence: widely distributed in Minnesota and throughout North America.

Plants with reddish-purple leaves are sometimes found. It appears that they were once planted in northern Minnesota dooryards. They still grow near old buildings.

Oxalis Family

65. Yellow Wood Sorrel (*O. stricta*). Also called Yellow Oxalis. A com-

65. Yellow Wood Sorrel. Summer.

66. Wild Geranium. Late spring; summer.

67. Fringed Polygala. Spring; summer.

Geranium Family

WILD GERANIUM (*Geranium*)

66. Wild Geranium (*G. maculatum*). Also called Crane's-bill. Perennial with a clump of palmately divided basal leaves and a leafy stem, usually 1 to 3 feet tall, topped by conspicuous, pale rosy-purple flowers. The flowers have 5 petals and are 1 to 2 inches across. When mature, the beaked seed pods split into 5 segments that suddenly coil upward, scattering the seeds. Often grows on roadsides. Occurrence: Minnesota — throughout, except in the southwest and northeast; general — temperate eastern North America.

Bicknell's Geranium (*G. bicknellii*) is an annual or biennial with similar, but smaller, flowers, about ½ inch across. It grows mostly in the northern forest areas, especially on disturbed soils. Stems are spreading and sprawling.

The cultivated geranium belongs to a different genus, *Pelargonium*, and comes from South Africa.

Milkwort Family

MILKWORT (*Polygala*)

67. Fringed Polygala (*P. paucifolia*). Also called Bird-on-the-Wing. A low perennial, usually 4 to 8 inches tall, of northern forests. The stem, which rises from a slender rootstalk, has 3 to 6 oval leaves near the top and a few much smaller leaves below. The solitary, rose-purple flower is quite distinctive. It is of irregular shape, and has a tufted fringe on the tip of the lower petal. Occurrence: Minnesota — mostly in the north and east on sandy soil where it often grows under pines; general — temperate eastern North America.

Milkwort Family

68. Seneca Snakeroot (*P. senega*). Perennial of dry prairies and open woods. The slender, unbranched, and usually clumped stems rise from a thick taproot. Generally they are 6 to 12 inches tall and end in a tapering cluster of small, white flowers. The roots contain bitter substances and oil of wintergreen that once had medicinal uses. Seneca Indians valued them for treating snakebite. The Potawatomi called this plant "Indian Head Dress," likening the flower-tipped stems to feathers of a subterranean warrior. Occurrence: Minnesota — throughout, except in the northeast and southwest; general — temperate eastern North America.

Spurge Family

SPURGE (*Euphorbia*)

69. Flowering Spurge (*E. corollata*). Erect, often clumped, perennial, usually 1 to 2 feet tall, with spreading clusters of white "flowers," each with 5 "petals." The apparent flower is really a much reduced inflorescence. The leaves have no teeth and are alternate, except for a whorl below the inflorescence. Juice is milky. Occurrence: Minnesota — old fields, open woods, and roadsides, mostly in the southeast; general — eastern U.S.

68. Seneca Snakeroot. Summer.

69. Flowering Spurge. Summer.

70. Leafy Spurge (*E. esula*). Erect perennial, usually 1 to 2 feet tall, with leafy stems ending in conspicuous, spreading clusters of yellow "flowers." The plants spread by horizontal rootstalks and often grow in patches. Juice is milky. Occurrence: of European origin, this aggressive plant is found throughout much of North America. In Minnesota it is officially designated as a "noxious weed."

The **Cypress Spurge** (*E. cyparissias*) has similar "flowers" but is lower growing, usually less than 1 foot tall, and has leaves mostly less than ¼ inch wide. Once planted in dooryards and cemeteries, it persists here and there but seldom produces seeds.

70. Leafy Spurge. Summer.

71. Spotted Touch-me-not. Summer.

Touch-me-not Family

TOUCH-ME-NOT (*Impatiens*)

71. Spotted Touch-me-not (*I. biflora*). Also called Spotted Jewelweed. Annual, often 2 to 3 feet tall, of wet places. The stems are watery and the leaves oval and coarsely toothed. The orange-yellow flower, commonly dotted with reddish brown, has a curved, forward pointing spur and hangs, nicely balanced, on a slender stalk. When the mature seed capsule is touched it explodes into curling segments, scattering the seeds. Occurrence: Minnesota — throughout; general — temperate eastern and central North America.

Pale Touch-me-not (*I. pallida*) is similar, but the base color of the flower is pale yellow and the short

88

spur is downward pointing. In Minnesota it grows mostly in moist places in the south.

St. John's-wort Family

ST. JOHN'S-WORT (*Hypericum*)

72. Common St. John's-wort (*H. perforatum*). Clumped, much branched perennial, usually 1 to 2 feet tall. The numerous yellow flowers have 5 spreading petals and many stamens. Leaves are opposite and dotted with internal oil-filled glands. Occurrence: Minnesota — mostly in the eastern portion along roads and in old pastures; general — a European species widely naturalized in North America.

Common St. John's-wort can be a troublesome pasture weed, often injurious if eaten by livestock. In Europe there is much folklore connected with it, including its use for treatment of weak eyes and as a talisman against thunder and witches.

St. John's-wort Family

73. Great St. John's-wort (*H. pyramidatum*). Robust perennial, usually 2 to 4 feet tall, of moist places, especially stream banks. The flowers are 1 to 2 inches across. They have 5 yellow petals and many conspicuous stamens. The reddish-brown seed pods are about 1 inch long. Leaves are opposite and dotted internally with oil-filled glands. Occurrence: Minnesota — mostly in the eastern half; general — temperate eastern North America.

This species has sometimes been used in folk medicine to treat respiratory troubles. There are several smaller native species.

89

72. Common St. John's-wort. Summer.

73. Great St. John's-wort. Summer.

74. Sweet White Violet. Spring; summer.

Violet Family

VIOLET (*Viola*)

74. Sweet White Violet (*V. pallens*). Low, tufted perennial of bogs, marshes, and shores. The small, white flowers are sweet-scented and marked with purple along the veins. Leaves are heart-shaped, all basal, and hairless. The plants spread by slender runners to form patches. Occurrence: Minnesota — mostly in the north and east; general — subarctic and temperate North America.

Several other species have white, sweet-scented flowers. *V. renifolia* has hairy, kidney-shaped leaves, *V. lanceolata*, narrow elongate leaves, and *V. incognita*, heart-shaped leaves that are hairy on one or both sides. All have only basal leaves and grow in moist places.

Violet Family

75. Yellow Violet (*V. pubescens*). The common yellow violet of deep woods and wooded edges. The flowers are borne at the top of a hairy, leafy stem. There are also 1 or 2 wide-bladed basal leaves. Occurrence: Minnesota — throughout; general — eastern temperate North America.

The **Smooth Yellow Violet** (var. *eriocarpa*) is similar but is hairless or nearly so, and usually has a

75. Yellow Violet. Spring; summer.

76. Canada Violet. Spring; summer.

clump of 2 or more leafy stems and more than 2 basal leaves. It is a plant of open woods and, sometimes, of meadows.

Violet Family

76. Canada Violet (*V. canadensis*). Woodland violet with conspicuous, white flowers, often tinged with pink or purple, and having yellowish centers. There are both basal and stem leaves with wide heart-shaped blades. Var. *rugulosa* has runners and rootstalks whereby it spreads to form patches. Occurrence: Minnesota – widespread but most common in the south; general – temperate North America.

Violet Family

77. Hooked Violet (*V. adunca*). A woodland violet, often of open pine forests. It has small, blue flowers, leaves usually less than 1 inch wide, and leafy stems covered with minute hairs. These hairs are visible under a hand lens. Stems are first erect and clumped but later trail and form patches. Occurrence: Minnesota – mostly in the north on sandy spots; general – temperate North America.

The **Dog Violet** (*V. conspersa*) has similar growth habits. However the leafy stems are hairless, or nearly so, and the flowers range from pale blue to nearly white. It grows in moist, sandy places.

77. Hooked Violet. Spring; summer.

78. Pansy Violet. Spring.

Violet Family

78. Pansy Violet (*V. pedata*). Characterized by deeply lobed leaves and flowers that are flat faced and often 1 inch across. The upper petals are deeper blue than the lower. Occurrence: Minnesota — mostly in the southeast and east central in open sandy places; general — temperate eastern North America.

The **Bird's-foot Violet** (*V. pedatifida*) also has divided leaves but grows in moist meadows and prairies. Petals are all the same shade of blue, and the lower petals are bearded on the inside near the base. It is found throughout much of Minnesota and temperate North America.

Violet Family

79. Downy Blue Violet (*V. sororia*). Also called Woolly Blue Violet. Commonest of blue violets with hairy basal leaves and no leafy stems. The leaf blades are toothed and about as long as wide. The leaves usually overtop the flowers. Occurrence: Minnesota — throughout in moist meadows and open woods; general — eastern temperate North America.

The **New England Violet** (*V. novae-angliae*) also has blue flowers and hairy basal leaves, but the leaf blades are markedly longer than wide. It is a plant of coarse soils and rocky places, especially along streams. In Minnesota it grows mostly in the north.

Violet Family

80. Missouri Violet (*V. missouriensis*). One of several species of blue violets with clumped basal leaves having heart-shaped blades that are hairless or nearly so. Flowers are pale blue and overtopped by the leaves. Occurrence: Minnesota — wooded floodplains in the south; general — central U.S.

The **Meadow Violet** (*V. papilionacea*) is a similar, nearly hairless

79. Downy Blue Violet. Spring.

plant of moist meadows, open woods, and dooryards, mostly in the south. It is the state flower of Wisconsin.

Several other species of stemless blue violets are separable from the foregoing only on the basis of technical characteristics. Hybrids between blue violet species are common.

80. Missouri Violet. Spring.

81. Western Prickly Pear. Summer.

Cactus Family

PRICKLY PEAR (*Opuntia*)

81. Western Prickly Pear (*O. humifusa*). The sprawling, jointed stem is made up of flat sections or "pads" armed with spines. Flowers are 2 to 3 inches across and have many pale yellow petals which may be reddish at the base. There are many stamens. The fruit is fleshy. Occurrence: Minnesota — open, usually rocky places in the south and west; general — central U.S.

The **Brittle Prickly Pear** (*O. fragilis*) has similar flowers, but the stem joints are long, nearly cylindrical, and the fruit is dry. A widely distributed western species of dry prairies and rocky places. The **Purple Cactus** (*Mammilaria vivipara*) is found in Minnesota only near the South Dakota border.

Loosestrife Family

PURPLE LOOSESTRIFE
(*Lythrum*)

82. Purple Loosestrife (*L. salicaria*). Also called Spiked Loosestrife. Stout perennial of marshes and shores. It is often 3 or 4 feet tall with conspicuous, elongate clusters of purple flowers. The flower has 6 crinkled petals. Leaves are opposite or whorled. Occurrence: Minnesota — naturalized in marshes and along streams in the Twin Cities area and less commonly elsewhere; general — a European species long established in eastern North America, perhaps originally introduced in the fleece of sheep.

Several color variants are grown as garden perennials. In the Lake Minnetonka area, west of Minneapolis, it has become abundant in many marshes since about 1940.

82. Purple Loosestrife. Summe

83. Fireweed. Summer.

84. Evening Primrose. Summer.

Evening Primrose Family

FIREWEED (*Epilobium*)

83. Fireweed (*E. angustifolium*). Also called Great Willow Herb. Clumped perennial of open and brushy uplands. It commonly grows 2 to 4 feet tall. The erect stems are usually reddish, have elongate, alternate leaves, and end in a tapering cluster of rose-purple flowers. Flowers have 4 petals and are 1 to 1½ inches across. The seeds, which are wind-borne by a tuft of hairs, are produced in slender pods that open from the top downward. Fireweed rapidly invades sites of forest fires and often becomes the most conspicuous plant. Occurrence: Minnesota — mostly in the east and north, often along roads; general — subarctic circumpolar, south to northern temperate U.S.

Evening Primrose Family

EVENING PRIMROSE
(*Oenothera*)

84. Evening Primrose (*O. biennis*). So called because the pale yellow flowers open in the evening and wither the following morning. They have 4 blunt petals that are often notched at the end. The plant is a biennial with a rosette of leaves the first year and in the second year an erect stem often 3 to 4 feet tall. Occurrence: Minnesota — old fields, roads, and other open places, mostly in the east and north; general — temperate eastern North America.

The **Rhombic Evening Primrose** (*O. rhombipetala*) of sandy areas in eastern and central Minnesota is similar but has wide petals that taper to a blunt point.

96

Evening Primrose Family

85. Toothed-leaved Evening Primrose (*O. serrulata*). Perennial of dry prairies. The somewhat woody stem, usually 1 to 2 feet tall, bears narrow leaves with widely spaced teeth. The yellow flowers are ½ to ¾ inch across. Unlike flowers of most other Evening Primroses, they remain open during the daylight hours. Occurrence: Minnesota — mostly in the south and west; general — temperate western North America.

Evening Primrose Family

86. Nuttall's Evening Primrose (*O. nuttallii*). The largest flowered, Minnesota Evening Primrose. The white or pinkish flowers are nearly 2 inches across. It grows up to 2 feet tall and has whitish bark and nodding flower buds. Occurrence: Minnesota — prairies, mostly in the northwest; general — temperate western North America.

85. Tooth-leaved Evening Primrose. Summer.

86. Nuttall's Evening Primrose. Summer.

87. Scarlet Gaura. Summer.

88. Enchanter's Nightshade. Summer.

GAURA (*Gaura*)

87. Scarlet Gaura (*G. coccinea*). Prairie plant with hairy, often branched stems, usually about a foot tall. The flowers have 4 pink to scarlet petals, are about ½ inch across, and are in an elongate inflorescence. Occurrence: Minnesota — mostly along the western border; general — temperate central and western North America.

Its name is from the Greek word for "showy."

Evening Primrose Family

ENCHANTER'S NIGHTSHADE (*Circaea*)

88. Enchanter's Nightshade (*C. quadrisulcata*). Woodland perennial, usually 1 to 2 feet tall, with opposite, oval leaves and slender clusters of small, white flowers. Flower parts are in 2's. The small, pear-shaped fruits are bristly with hooked hairs that cling to clothing. Occurrence: Minnesota — common in woods; general — widespread in eastern North America. Also in Asia.

Smaller Enchanter's Nightshade (*C. alpina*) is similar but is 3 to 8 inches tall and grows in wet woods and swamps, mostly in the north.

The enchanter referred to in the name is the "clinging" enchantress Circe, who detained Ulysses on his travels.

Aralia Family

ARALIA (*Aralia*)

89. Wild Sarsaparilla (*A. nudicaulis*). Common perennial of forests. The

89. Wild Sarsaparilla. Summer.

leafy plants, about 1 foot tall, are really spreading, 3-part compound leaves, each on an upright stalk. They rise from rootstalks that also bear leafless stems ending in 3 clusters (umbels) of greenish-white flowers. In late summer these develop into purplish-black berries. Occurrence: Minnesota — throughout in wooded areas but most common in the north; general — temperate North America.

The berries are eaten by bears and foxes, and the aromatic rootstalks were once used in folk medicine and for flavoring root beer.

90. American Spikenard. Summer.

Aralia Family

90. American Spikenard (*A. racemosa*). Stout perennial of rich woods. Stems are often 3 to 6 feet long and somewhat arching. It has large, spreading, compound leaves with many leaflets. The small, white flowers are in an elongate, much-branched inflorescence. They are followed by small purple berries. Occurrence: Minnesota — throughout in woods; general — temperate eastern North America.

The stout root is aromatic and once had medicinal uses. It was also used to flavor root beer. The berries have been used for jelly.

Aralia Family

GINSENG (*Panax*)

91. Ginseng (*P. quinquefolium*). The Chinese consider the spindle-shaped root, which sometimes has nearly human form, to be of great medicinal value and in America the roots have long been collected, dried, and exported to China. Ginseng is now very rare in the wild, but it is sometimes cultivated. It is a perennial of rich hardwood forests and usually grows 1 to 1½ feet tall. The stem ends in a group of 3 palmately compound leaves, each with 5 spreading leaflets. A cluster of small, white

91. Ginseng. Summer.

flowers rises at the junction of the leaves. In fall there is a cluster of bright red berries. Occurrence: Minnesota — mostly in the southeast and central; general — temperate eastern North America.

Parsley Family

CARROT (*Daucus*)

92. Wild Carrot (*D. carota*). Also called Queen Anne's Lace. The ancestor of the garden carrot. This European biennial grows on roadsides, in old fields, and in waste places. The stem, usually 1 to 2 feet tall, bears elongate, much divided leaves and conspicuous, flat clusters (compound umbels) of small, white flowers. The center flower of the umbel is often purple. The umbels face the sky during the day but bend downward at night. When in fruit, the branches of the umbel curve upward in a bird's-nest pattern. Occurrence: widely distributed as a weedy plant throughout Minnesota and elsewhere in North America.

Parsley Family

WATER HEMLOCK (*Cicuta*)

93. Water Hemlock (*C. maculata*). Also called Musquash Root and Spotted Cowbane. Our most poisonous plant. It contains a poisonous resin, cicutatoxin, concentrated in the elongate tubers at the base of the stem. Ingestion of a small piece of tuber is sufficient to cause convulsions and death in humans. Water Hemlock grows in marshes, roadside ditches, and along streams. It is usually 3 to 6 feet tall and has large, compound leaves with toothed leaflets. The small, white flowers are grouped in compound clusters

(umbels) that are several inches across. Occurrence: Minnesota — throughout; general — subarctic and temperate North America.

Cattle can eat the leaves and stems, fresh or as hay, apparently without harm, but they have been killed by pulling up the plants and eating the roots.

92. Wild Carrot. Summer.

93. Water Hemlock. Summer.

101

Parsley Family

WATER PARSNIP (*Sium*)

94. Water Parsnip (*S. suave*). Perennial, usually 2 to 4 feet tall, of wet marshes, quiet waters, and shores. It is remarkable for variation in the shape of the leaves. Aerial leaves are pinnately compound with quite ordinary, elongate, toothed leaflets, but submerged leaves are much cut and divided. The small, white flowers are in spreading, compound umbels. Occurrence: Minnesota — throughout, often abundant in forest ponds; general — subarctic North America south through much of U.S.

Water Parsnip has sometimes poisoned cattle.

94. Water Parsnip. Summer.

95. Cow Parsnip. Summer.

Parsley Family

COW PARSNIP (*Heracleum*)

95. Cow Parsnip (*H. lanatum*). Giant herb, often growing to a height of 8 feet or more. It has large, compound leaves with 3 main divisions. Leaflets are hairy beneath, coarsely toothed, and often lobed and heart-shaped at the base. The white flowers are in large, flat clusters (compound umbels). Individual flowers at the edge of the umbel have longer outer than inner petals. Occurrence: Minnesota — throughout on rich, moist soils, especially along forest edges and roads; general — subarctic and much of temperate North America. Also in Siberia.

Heracleum refers to Herakles, the mighty and muscular doer of Greek odd jobs. The Menomini Indians used this plant as a charm to ensure success in deer hunting.

102

96. Golden Alexanders. Spring; summer.

Parsley Family

GOLDEN ALEXANDERS (*Zizia*)

96. Golden Alexanders (*Z. aurea*). Late spring wild flower of open, grassy places. It is a perennial, usually 1 to 2 feet tall. The small, yellow flowers are in a flat-topped cluster (compound umbel), and all the leaves are compound with elongate leaflets. Occurrence: Minnesota — moist meadows, prairies, and brushy places throughout; general — eastern U.S. and adjacent Canada.

The **Heart-leaved Alexanders** (*Z. cordata*) is similar but has heart-shaped basal leaves. It grows in moist grassy places and open woods.

The name *Alexanders* is borrowed from a similar European plant.

103

97. Wild Parsnip. Late spring; summer.

Parsley Family

PARSNIP (*Pastinaca*)

97. Wild Parsnip (*P. sativa*). Erect biennial, usually 2 to 4 feet tall, with flat clusters of many small, yellow flowers. The leaves are pinnately compound with leaflets that are toothed and lobed. It is the wild form of the garden parsnip, but the taproot is usually woody and inedible. Occurrence: A European plant frequently naturalized along roads and in waste places, especially in the vicinity of towns and farmsteads where parsnips have been raised as a vegetable.

Certain individuals are sensitive to parsnips and develop dermatitis from contact with the leaves and flowers.

98. Bunchberry. Spring; summer.

Dogwood Family

BUNCHBERRY (*Cornus*)

98. Bunchberry (*C. canadensis*). A common, low plant of northern woods and bogs, often in sandy or rocky places. Near the top of the upright stem, usually 3 to 6 inches tall, is a whorl of 4 to 6 spreading, elliptical leaves. Above these is a stalked cluster of small flowers, surrounded by 4 white bracts that resemble petals. In late summer the inflorescence becomes a "bunch" of bright red berries. The plant has elongate underground stems by which it spreads and forms patches. Occurrence: Minnesota — in the north and east; general — subarctic North America south to northern U.S. Also in eastern Asia.

Sandalwood Family

BASTARD TOADFLAX
(*Comandra*)

99. Bastard Toadflax (*C. umbellata*). Low perennial of prairies, meadows, and open woods. The erect, leafy stems, usually 6 to 12 inches tall, end in a cluster of small, white flowers. The stems rise from spreading rootstalks and usually grow in patches. Leaves are oblong to elliptical. Bastard Toadflax is a semiparasite, its roots attached to those of other plants. Occurrence: Minnesota — throughout, usually in meadows; general — temperate North America.

The similar **Northern Bastard Toadflax** (*C. livida*) is found in northeastern Minnesota and on Isle Royale. It has juicy, orange-red fruits.

99. Bastard Toadflax. Spring; summer.

100. Wild Ginger. Spring.

Birthwort Family

WILD GINGER (*Asarum*)

100. Wild Ginger (*A. canadense*). Low woodland perennial. It has a pair of hairy, heart- or kidney-shaped leaves at the end of an elongate and rather thick rootstalk. The solitary flower is at ground level, between the stalks of the paired leaves. It is dark red or brownish and has 3 triangular calyx lobes. The rootstalk has a mild ginger flavor and has been used in Indian and folk medicine. Occurrence: Minnesota — throughout in hardwood forests; general — temperate eastern North America.

101. Swamp Smartweed. Summer.

Smartweed Family

SMARTWEED (*Polygonum*)

101. Swamp Smartweed (*P. coccineum*). Perennial of marshes and shores, sometimes growing in shallow water. Usually it is 1 to 3 feet tall. It has small, rosy flowers in elongate clusters and alternate, hairy leaves. There is a tubular collar around the stem above the base of each leaf stalk. Occurrence: Minnesota — widely distributed in wet, open places; general — temperate North America.

The **Water Smartweed** (*P. natans*), also perennial, often grows in shallow water. Here it has floating leaves that are shiny green above and red beneath. The rosy flowers are in short, blunt clusters.

Smartweed Family

102. Dock-leaved Smartweed (*P. lapathifolium*). Erect annual, often 3 to 4 feet tall, with long, nodding clusters of small, white to rose flowers. The elongate leaves taper to both ends and the stem is swollen at the nodes and often branched. Occurrence: Minnesota — widely distribut-

ed on damp soils subject to flooding and as a weed on moist, cultivated soils; general — northern U.S. and adjacent Canada. Also in Eurasia.

There are several similar annual smartweeds. The **Pennsylvania Smartweed** (*P. pensylvanicum*) has blunt, upright clusters of pink or white flowers. It often grows in old fields where the soil is sandy.

102. Dock-leaved Smartweed. Summer.

103. Fringed Bindweed. Summer.

Smartweed Family

103. Fringed Bindweed (*P. cilinode*). Perennial of open woods, thickets, or rocky places. It has twining, trailing, or sprawling stems that are usually reddish and hairy. Leaves are heart-shaped or arrow-head-shaped, and the numerous white flowers are in loose, fringelike clusters. Occurrence: Minnesota — mostly in the north and especially common in the northeast; general — temperate North America.

104. Wild Four-o'clock. Summer.

105. Spring Beauty. Spring.

Four-o'clock Family

UMBRELLA-WORT (*Mirabilis*)

104. Wild Four-o'clock (*M. nyctaginea*). Also called Heart-leaved Umbrella-wort. Erect perennial, usually 1 to 3 feet tall, with forking stems and stalked, heart-shaped leaves. The funnel-shaped, rosy flowers rise from a saucerlike structure, the "umbrella." The flowers open in the afternoon and usually wilt by noon of the following day. Stems are markedly noded, tend to be 4-sided, and are hairless or nearly so. Occurrence: Minnesota — throughout in dry, open places, often appearing uninvited in sunny dooryards and gardens; general — much of temperate North America.

Purslane Family

SPRING BEAUTY (*Claytonia*)

105. Spring Beauty (*C. virginica*). A well-named, spring wild flower of damp woods and clearings. The short stems, 6 to 10 inches tall, and the narrow, elongate leaves are both somewhat fleshy. Flowers are pink and in loose clusters. They have 5 petals which are veined with deeper pink. Occurrence: Minnesota — in the east but most common in the southeast; general — eastern U.S. and adjacent Canada.

The **Broad-leaved Spring Beauty** (*C. caroliniana*), which has wider and distinctly stalked leaves, is known in Minnesota from southern St. Louis County.

106. Water Chickweed. Summer.

107. Grove Sandwort. Spring.

Pink Family

CHICKWEED (*Stellaria*)

106. Water Chickweed (*S. aquatica*). Weak stemmed, but robust, spreading perennial of damp places, especially along streams. Often forms patches a foot or more across. The oval, pointed leaves are opposite on the hairy stems, and the white flowers are on forking, upright branches. Each flower is about ½ inch across and has 5 deeply notched petals. Occurrence: Minnesota — occasional throughout; general — a native of Europe but widespread in temperate North America.

Several other chickweeds have smaller flowers. The **Common**

Chickweed (*S. media*) is a weedy annual of gardens and lawns. *Stellaria* is Latin for "little star," referring to the flower, and the "chick" in chickweed alludes to the former use of the tiny seeds as food for caged song birds.

Pink Family

SANDWORT (*Arenaria*)

107. Grove Sandwort (*A. lateriflora*). Low perennial of woods and brushy places. The slender, erect stem, usually less than 8 inches tall, has opposite leaves and 5-petaled, white flowers in an upright, forking cluster. The plants have running rootstalks and sometimes grow in patches. Occurrence: Minnesota — throughout, often on sandy soil; general — subarctic circumpolar, south in North America to northern U.S.

Pink Family

CAMPION (*Lychnis*)

108. White Campion (*L. alba*). Common roadside plant with white flowers. Usually 1 to 3 feet tall. It has opposite leaves and loose clusters of flowers, each about ¾ inch across and with 5 notched petals that have a flaplike "claw" at the base. Male and female flowers are on different plants. Female flowers have a rounded, bladderlike calyx and the male flowers a tubular calyx. In the center of the female flower are 5 elongate styles. Occurrence: a European annual or biennial widely distributed in Minnesota and elsewhere in North America.

Campion is an old name referring to fields where such plants often grow.

108. White Campion. Summer.

109. Starry Campion. Summer.

Pink Family

CAMPION, CATCHFLY (*Silene*)

109. Starry Campion (*S. stellata*). Perennial, commonly 1 to 2 feet tall, growing in woods and brushy places. Leaves are in whorls of 4, and the white flowers are in conspicuous, open clusters. The flowers have 5 fringed petals. Occurrence: Minnesota — mostly in the south; general — eastern U.S.

The **Night-flowering Catchfly** (*S. noctiflora*) is much like White Campion but has sticky, hairy stems and white or pale pink flowers with 3 rather than 5 styles. The flowers open late in the afternoon. This widely distributed plant is of European origin. Often grows in shady places.

The sticky stems of some species catch and hold small insects. Silene was a bibulous Greek god who was covered with sticky, alcoholic foam and had a potbelly like a campion pod.

Pink Family

BOUNCING BET (*Saponaria*)

110. Bouncing Bet (*S. officinalis*). A European perennial that escaped from pioneer gardens to nearby roadsides. The showy clusters of pink flowers top leafy stems that are commonly 1 to 2 feet tall. Occasionally there are plants with semidouble flowers that range in color from white to rosy lilac. The

112

110. Bouncing Bet. Late spring; summer.

plant, especially the rootstalk, contains saponin which produces slippery suds in water. It was once used as a natural detergent for washing fine fabrics and is still used occasionally in museums for cleaning old tapestries. Occurrence: widely naturalized in Minnesota and elsewhere in temperate North America.

It makes a showy garden perennial but is aggressive and spreading.

Heath Family

INDIAN PIPE (*Monotropa*)

111. Indian Pipe (*M. uniflora*). A remarkable forest plant, usually 3 to 6 inches tall, with upright stems and nodding, pipe-shaped flowers that look as if they were modeled from white wax. Occasionally they are pink, and they always turn black if picked and dried. When in clumps, all the flowers often face the same way. Indian Pipe lives in partnership with a fungus and may also be parasitic on other plants. The stems rise from a mass of thickened roots. Occurrence: Minnesota — northern forests, often in dense shade; general — widely distributed in North America. Also in eastern Asia.

111. Indian Pipe. Summer.

112. Common Shinleaf. Summer.

Heath Family

SHINLEAF (*Pyrola*)

112. Common Shinleaf (*P. elliptica*). Low plant, less than 8 inches tall, of dry woods. It has a tuft of thin, elliptical leaves and erect clusters of nodding, white flowers. These have 5 petals and are fragrant. Occur-rence: Minnesota — mostly in the eastern half, often under hardwood trees; general — much of temperate North America. Also in eastern Asia.

In Minnesota there are several other pyrolas with erect clusters of white or greenish flowers. The **One-flowered Shinleaf** (*Moneses uniflora*) is a related low plant with a solitary, nodding, white flower, It is common in moist woods and bogs in the north.

Heath Family

113. Pink Shinleaf (*P. asarifolia*). The nodding flowers are pink or purple in an elongate, upright cluster. Leaves are basal. They are thick and shiny and have round or kidney-shaped blades. The plants often grow in patches. Occurrence: Minnesota — mostly in the northern forested area, especially in the northeast; general — subarctic to temperate North America.

Heath Family

LABRADOR TEA (*Ledum*)

114. Labrador Tea (*L. groenlandicum*). Common low shrub of open

113. Pink Shinleaf. Summer.

114. Labrador Tea. Summer.

and wooded bogs. Usually 1 to 3 feet tall. Twigs are densely hairy. The elongate, evergreen leaves have rolled margins and are densely hairy beneath. Flowers are white with 5 petals and are arranged in spreading, somewhat rounded clusters. Occurrence: Minnesota — in the north and central, especially in bogs of the coniferous forest area; general — subarctic North America south to northern U.S.

The leaves have been used as a substitute for tea.

Heath Family

LAUREL (*Kalmia*)

115. Swamp Laurel (*K. polifolia*). Low shrub of wet bogs and muskegs. Here it usually grows with other small shrubs of the Heath Family. It has leathery, opposite leaves and loose clusters of attractive rose-purple flowers, each with 5 spreading petals united at the base. Occurrence: Minnesota — forested areas of the north and central, most common in the northeast; general — subarctic North America south to northern U.S.

The leaves are poisonous to cattle and sheep but are tough and usually not eaten. *Kalmia* honors Peter Kalm (1715-1779), Swedish botanist and early traveler in North America.

115. Swamp Laurel. Summer.

116. Bog Rosemary. Summer.

Heath Family

BOG ROSEMARY (*Andromeda*)

116. Bog Rosemary (*A. glaucophylla*). Low shrub, less than 2 feet tall, of wetter parts of bogs and muskegs. The alternate leaves are evergreen, narrow, and have rolled edges. The white or pinkish flowers are in small clusters on the upper part of the stem. They are urn-shaped, with 5 united petals. The leaves, like those of *Kalmia* and probably *Ledum*, are poisonous to sheep. Occurrence: Minnesota — in the north and central, usually growing with other bog heaths; general — subarctic south to northern U.S.

In Greek mythology Andromeda was an Ethiopian princess who was chained to a rock by the sea and rescued from a sea monster by Perseus.

117. Leatherleaf. Spring.

Heath Family

LEATHERLEAF (*Chamaedaphne*)

117. Leatherleaf (*C. calyculata*). Common low shrub, 2 to 4 feet tall, of marshes and muskegs. It often grows with the 3 preceding shrubby members of the Heath Family. The nodding, white flowers are in the axils of the upper leaves. They have 5 fused petals and are bell-shaped, with a narrow throat. Leaves are thick and evergreen and are alternately arranged on the much branched stems. Occurrence: Minnesota — common in bogs, especially in the coniferous forest region of the north; general — arctic to temperate regions in both North America and Eurasia.

118. Wintergreen. Summer.

Heath Family

WINTERGREEN (*Gaultheria*)

118. Wintergreen (*G. procumbens*). Also called Checkerberry. Low plant of open woods, usually in sandy or rocky places. The short, erect, branchlike stems rise from slender, trailing or underground stems. Leaves are toothed, elliptical, evergreen, and shiny. The nodding, white flowers are followed by edible, red berries that sometimes survive the winter. The entire plant has a strong odor of oil of wintergreen (methyl salicylate). Indians and early explorers made a tea from the leaves that was considered beneficial for rheumatism. Occurrence: Minnesota — mostly in the north and east in coniferous forest regions; general — temperate eastern North America.

Trailing Arbutus (*Epigaea repens*), another low, trailing plant

118a. Wintergreen in fruit. Autumn.

of the Heath Family, has pink flowers and ovate, usually hairy leaves. It grows on sandy soil in the north, but is uncommon.

Heath Family

LINGENBERRY (*Vaccinium*)

119. Lingenberry (*V. vitis-idaea*). Also called Mountain Cranberry. Low, branched shrub, usually less than 6 inches tall, of mossy bogs and sometimes moist, upland sites. The small leaves are elliptical, thick, and evergreen, and the flowers pink and bell-shaped. They are followed in late summer by red berries that are tart and much like cranberries but have a distinctive flavor. M. L. Fernald, noted botanist at Harvard, was of the opinion that lingenberries, not wild grapes, were the *vinber* from which the Vikings derived the name Vinland. Occurrence: Minnesota — occasional in the north and northeast; general — widely distributed in arctic North America, including the east coast of Canada. Circumboreale.

119. Lingenberry in fruit. Autumn.

120. Swamp Candles. Summer.

Primrose Family

LOOSESTRIFE (*Lysimachia*)

120. Swamp Candles (*L. terrestris*). Also called Yellow or Bulb-bearing Loosestrife. Erect perennial of bogs and marshes. It is usually 1 to 2 feet tall. The stem bears opposite, hairless leaves and 5-petaled, yellow flowers in an erect, spikelike cluster. On the petals are dark markings. Reddish bulblets often develop in the leaf axils. Occurrence: Minnesota — mostly in the east and north; general — temperate eastern North America.

119

Primrose Family

121. Moneywort (*L. nummularia*). Low, trailing perennial with pale yellow flowers and opposite, nearly circular leaves. The bell-shaped flowers have 5 petals dotted with dark red. Moneywort was planted in pioneer gardens and in cemeteries to cover graves and is still used as ground cover in shady places. The specific name, *nummularia*, means "coinlike" and refers to the round leaves. Moneywort is a native of Europe that is widely naturalized in eastern North America.

Primrose Family

122. Fringed Loosestrife (*L. ciliata*). Erect, often branched perennial of damp thickets, marshes, and shores. It is usually 1 to 2 feet tall. Leaves are opposite with pointed, oval blades and the leaf stalks are fringed on the upper angles with curly, white hairs. The flowers are yellow with 5 wide, pointed petals. Each flower is on a slender stalk. Occurrence: Minnesota — throughout; general — temperate North America.

121. Moneywort. Summer.

122. Fringed Loosestrife. Summer.

120

Primrose Family

123. Tufted Loosestrife (*L. thyrsiflora*). A perennial of open and wooded swamps. The erect stems, usually 1 to 2 feet tall, have elongate, opposite leaves and stalked clusters or "tufts" of small yellow flowers in the leaf axils. Each flower has 5 narrow petals on which are dark markings. Occurrence: Minnesota — throughout, sometimes in shallow water; general — subarctic circumpolar, in North America south to northern U.S.

Primrose Family

STAR FLOWER (*Trientalis*)

124. Star Flower (*T. americana*). Low perennial of moist woods and bogs, often growing among mosses. The slender, upright stem is usually less than 8 inches tall and rises from an elongate rootstalk. The stem is topped by a whorl of leaves of various sizes and by starry, white flowers on slender stalks. Usually the flowers have 7 petals and 7 stamens. Occurrence: Minnesota — mostly in the north and central; general — subarctic south to temperate U.S.

Plants with flower parts in 7's are very rare. In the Linnaean "Sexual System" of plant classification Star Flower was one of the few plants in Class Heptandra, i.e., flowers with 7 stamens.

123. Tufted Loosestrife. Summer.

124. Star Flower. Summer.

125. Closed Gentian. Autumn.

126. Yellowish Gentian. Autumn.

Gentian Family

GENTIAN (*Gentiana*)

125. Closed Gentian (*G. andrewsii*). Also called Bottle Gentian. Perennial with upright stems, usually 1 to 2 feet tall, that end in clusters of club- or bottle-shaped, blue flowers. The top of the flower is closed or nearly so, making the interior available only to large insects such as bumblebees, which can push the petals apart. The toothless leaves are opposite with a pair of nerves in addition to the midrib. Occurrence: Minnesota — throughout, in moist, undisturbed open or somewhat shaded areas; general — temperate eastern North America.

Gentian Family

126. Yellowish Gentian (*G. flavida*). Perennial with upright stems, 1 to 2 feet tall, ending in a cluster of greenish white to yellowish white flowers, 1 to 1½ inches long. The opposite leaves have 3 nerves and are stalkless and somewhat clasp the stem. Occurrence: Minnesota — uncommon and local, mostly in the southeast. The photograph was taken on a railroad right-of-way in Deephaven, Hennepin County; general — eastern U.S. and adjacent Canada.

Gentian Family

127. Downy Gentian (*G. puberula*). Perennial of dry prairies and open woods. The stems, usually 6 to 12 inches long and often somewhat sprawling, end in one or more dark blue or blue-purple flowers. Each has 5 petals that are spreading above but joined below to form a tube. Occurrence: Minnesota — on prairies in the south and west; general — temperate central North America.

The name gentian harks back to Gentius, king of ancient Illyria, who is said to have discovered the medicinal value of gentian root.

122

Gentian Family

128. Fringed Gentian (*G. crinita*).
Perhaps the most beautiful of
autumn wild flowers. This biennial prefers moist, limy sites, such
as calcareous bogs, shores, and seepage areas. The plant, usually 8 to
24 inches tall, is often branched
above and has opposite leaves. It
has conspicuous, blue flowers with
4 spreading petals that are fringed
at the end and part way down the
sides. The petals are twisted together when the flower is closed.
Occurrence: Minnesota — mostly in
the east and north, but local;
general — temperate eastern North
America.

127. Downy Gentian. Autumn.

128. Fringed Gentian. Autumn.

129. Buckbean. Summer.

130. Common Dogbane. Summer.

Gentian Family

BUCKBEAN (*Menyanthes*)

129. Buckbean (*M. trifoliata*). Low perennial of bogs, swamps, and lake margins, sometimes growing in shallow water. Leaves are shiny, have 3 leaflets, and are usually clumped at the end of a thick rootstalk. The white, 5-petaled flowers are in an elongate, upright cluster, and the upper surface of the petals is covered with curved hairs. Occurrence: Minnesota — wooded northern two-thirds; general — subarctic circumpolar, south in North America to northern U.S.

The juice is bitter, as it is in many members of the Gentian Family. Gentian root, especially that of the European *G. lutea*, has long been used medicinally as a tonic and also as one of the components of "bitters" in mixed drinks.

Dogbane Family

DOGBANE (*Apocynum*)

130. Common Dogbane (*A. androsaemifolium*). Also called Spreading Dogbane. Bushy perennial, usually 1 to 2 feet tall, with spreading branches. A plant of roadsides, fields, and open woods, it has loose clusters of small, pink to nearly white, bell-shaped flowers. The elliptical leaves are opposite and the plant contains milky juice. Seeds with a tuft of hair at one end are produced in paired pods. Occurrence: Minnesota — throughout; general — widely distributed in North America.

Small insects are sometimes held fast in the blossoms by the

124

sticky pollen. Indians twisted the fibrous outer bark to make thread and bow strings. Both this and the following species have sometimes poisoned herbivorous animals. Dogbane is an ancient name, but we know of no dogs poisoned by it.

Dogbane Family

131. Indian Hemp (*A. cannabimum*). Robust perennial of moist roadsides and open places. Often grows 3 to 4 feet tall, with erect stems that are branched toward the top. The elliptical leaves are opposite on short stalks, and the small, white flowers are erect in rather compact clusters. Occurrence: Minnesota — mostly in the south and west; general — temperate North America.

The plant contains a glucoside and is reported to have been used by Indians as a fish poison. Its fibrous stems were used by Indians to make cordage and fish nets.

Sessile-leaved Dogbane (*A. sibiricum*) of prairies is similar but it has leaves that clasp the stem or are on very short stalks.

131. Indian Hemp. Summer.

132. Common Milkweed. Summer.

Milkweed Family

MILKWEED (*Asclepias*)

132. Common Milkweed (*A. syriaca*). Robust perennial of open places; it is often 3 to 4 feet tall and grows in patches. The erect, hairy stems have elliptical, opposite leaves and stalked clus-

133. Showy Milkweed. Summer.

ters of purplish-green flowers. The upright petals are hoodlike and rounder and shorter than the sepals below them. Juice is milky. The flat seeds are windborne by a tuft of silky hairs. Occurrence: Minnesota — throughout, but uncommon in the northeast; general — temperate eastern North America.

Stems with open pods, from which the seeds have been released, are gathered for winter bouquets. Young stems, pods, and flower buds have sometimes been cooked like asparagus. The flowers are rich in nectar and attract many insects.

Milkweed Family

133. Showy Milkweed (*A. speciosa*). Similar to the Common Milkweed but the flowers have longer and more tapering, upright petals (hoods) and an abundance of woolly hairs. Occurrence: Minnesota — prairies in the west; general — temperate western North America.

Stem fibers of this and some other milkweeds were used by Indians to make cords and rope.

126

Milkweed Family

134. Swamp Milkweed (*A. incarnata*). Common, erect perennial, usually 3 to 4 feet tall, of marshes and shores. It has clusters of pink to rose-purple flowers, tapering, opposite leaves, and milky juice. Often the entire plant is reddish. Occurrence: Minnesota — throughout; general — temperate North America.

This milkweed is quite ornamental and is sometimes grown in gardens. The root was used medicinally by the Chippewa Indians.

Milkweed Family

135. Butterflyweed (*A. tuberosa*). Also called Pleurisy Root. One of the brightest and most conspicuous of northern wild flowers. Stems, usually 1 to 2 feet tall, are often clumped and bear narrow, alternate leaves and spreading clusters (umbels) of flowers ranging from bright yellow to blazing orange. Herbage is hairy. This plant, unlike other milkweeds, has no milky juice. Occurrence: Minnesota — mostly in the south and

134. Swamp Milkweed. Summer.

east in open places, often on sand; general — eastern and central North America.

Butterflyweed makes a showy garden perennial and can be raised from seed or root cuttings. The thick root was used in Indian and folk medicine, especially for lung and chest complaints.

135. Butterflyweed. Late spring; summer.

136. Whorled Milkweed. Summer.

137. Poke Milkweed. Summer.

Milkweed Family

136. Whorled Milkweed (*A. verticillata*). A common, white flowered perennial of dry prairies, roadsides, and other open places. It often grows in patches on poor or shallow soils. The erect stems, usually 6 to 15 inches tall, bear many slender leaves in whorls of 3 to 6 and umbels of small, white or greenish-white flowers. It is poisonous to sheep. Occurrence: Minnesota — throughout, except in the northeast; general — eastern U.S. and adjacent Canada.

Milkweed Family

137. Poke Milkweed (*A. exaltata*). A beautiful milkweed of moist woods and wooded edges. The stem, usually 2 to 4 feet tall, has opposite leaves that are thin, elliptical, and tapering at both ends. The white or pinkish flowers are borne on slender stalks and are arranged in spreading, often drooping, clusters. Occurrence: Minnesota — mostly in the southeast; general — eastern U.S.

Morning-glory Family

BINDWEED (*Convolvulus*)

138. Hedge Bindweed (*C. sepium*). Perennial twining vine, growing up to 10 feet long on brushy sites, old fences, and sometimes in grassy or marshy places. The large, white or pink flowers are bell-shaped and about 2 inches across. They open in the morning and close in the afternoon. Leaves are arrowhead-shaped and alternate on the stem. Occurrence: Minnesota — throughout; general — widely

138. Hedge Bindweed. Summer.

distributed in eastern and central North America.

Creeping Jenny (*C. arvensis*), also called Field Bindweed, is similar but with smaller flowers. It has creeping or low-climbing stems and hairy leaves. The flowers have a waxy, almond odor. This native of Europe is a weedy perennial of open places.

Morning-glory Family ·

139. Upright Bindweed (*C. spithameus*). Slender, erect or feebly twining perennial of open woods and fields, often on sandy soil. The plant is usually less than a foot tall and has alternate, hairy leaves. The white, bell-shaped flowers are about 1½ inches wide when fully open. Occurrence: Minnesota — east and north, mostly in coniferous forests; general — temperate eastern North America.

139. Upright Bindweed. Summer.

129

Morning-glory Family

DODDER (*Cuscuta*)

140. Dodder (*Cuscuta* spp.). Parasitic plants without green leaves and with slender, yellow or reddish stems that twine around upright stems of other green plants. The small flowers, in compact clusters, are followed by rounded seed pods. Dodder begins growth in late spring from a seed in the soil. However, the vine soon attaches itself to stems of other plants by rootlike structures (haustoria) through which it taps the food-conducting tissue of its host. In moist, lowland forests Dodder often spreads over large patches of herbs. Occurrence: several species occur in Minnesota and are widespread in North America.

140. Dodder. Summer; autumn.

141. Wild Blue Phlox. Spring.

142. Downy Phlox. Spring.

Phlox Family

PHLOX (*Phlox*)

141. Wild Blue Phlox (*P. divaricata*). Also called Wood Phlox. A perennial of rich woods. The stems, usually about a foot tall, rise from slender rootstalks. The plants when in bloom form pale blue clumps and patches. Occasionally plants have white or purplish flowers. The flowers are in flat-topped clusters and are faintly fragrant. The flower has 5 spreading petals that are united below to form a tube. Occurrence: Minnesota – most common in the southeastern third; general – eastern temperate North America.

Wood Phlox does well in a shady garden spot if given good soil and plenty of water.

Phlox Family

142. Downy Phlox (*P. pilosa*). Also called Prairie Phlox and, by pioneers, Sweet William. Perennial of moist meadows, prairies, and open woods. Stems, which are often clumped, have opposite leaves that are narrow and tapering. The flowers are pink or rosy, often with a darker center or "eye." They are arranged in a spreading cluster. Occurrence: Minnesota – throughout except in the northeast; general – a typical meadow and prairie plant throughout eastern temperate North America.

Prairie Phlox well exemplifies the name phlox, which is Greek for "flame."

131

143. Virginia Waterleaf. Spring.

Waterleaf Family

WATERLEAF (*Hydrophyllum*)

143. Virginia Waterleaf (*H. virginicum*). Common perennial of upland woods and shady floodplains. It generally grows 1 to 2 feet tall and spreads by rootstalks. The large basal and stem leaves are deeply divided into irregularly toothed and sometimes lobed segments. Often the leaves have white splotches on them. These were once thought to contain water, hence the name. The white to purple bell-shaped flowers are in rather dense clusters, each flower having 5 protruding stamens which give the ·clusters a fringed appearance. Occurrence: Minnesota — throughout, except in extreme northeast; general — temperate eastern North America.

Borage Family

PUCCOON (*Lithospermum*)

144. Carolina Puccoon (*L. caroliniense*). A bright orange-yellow wild flower of late spring. The erect, leafy stems, usually 1 to 2 feet tall, rise from a thick perennial root. Stems are topped by a spreading cluster of flowers. Each flower is about ¾ inch across and has 5 petals united toward the base. Indians used the root to make a red dye. The word puccoon is of Algonkian origin, meaning "blood." Occurrence: Minnesota — in the southeast and central, especially on the east-central sand plain; general — much of temperate and southern U.S.

The **Hoary Puccoon** (*L. canescens*) is similar but has flowers

144. Carolina Puccoon. Spring.

about ½ inch across and herbage that is densely covered with short, soft hairs. It is a fairly common plant of prairies, meadows, and open woods in Minnesota and eastern U.S.

Borage Family

FORGET-ME-NOT (*Myosotis*)

145. Forget-me-not (*M. scorpioides*). This European plant sometimes escapes from cultivation and becomes naturalized along streams and in seepage areas. It tolerates some shade and can grow in shallow water. The bright blue flowers are ¼ to ½ inch across. It is perennial with creeping, rooting stems from which rise short, erect flowering stalks. Occurrence: Minnesota — in the east, common along Minnehaha Creek below the falls; general — throughout temperate North America.

The **Bay Forget-me-not** (*M. laxa*) is similar but with smaller flowers and usually it is not creeping. It is known from moist places in north-central Minnesota.

145. Forget-me-not. Spring.

133

146. Virginia Bluebell. Spring.

Borage Family

BLUEBELL, LUNGWORT
(*Mertensia*)

146. Virginia Bluebell (*M. virginica*). Also called Virginia Cowslip. A perennial mostly 1 to 2 feet tall with leafy, often clumped, stems. The nodding, blue flowers, about 1 inch long, are in a loose cluster. Buds are pink. The blunt, hairless leaves are without teeth and have a bluish cast. Occurrence: Minnesota — moist woods and river bottoms in the southeast; general —

eastern U.S. south to Alabama. It is often planted in gardens and blossoms along with daffodils.

The **Tall Lungwort** (*M. paniculata*), locally called Bluebell, has similar blue flowers, but the leaves are pointed and hairy on both sides. In Minnesota it is found mostly in the northeast, especially along Lake Superior. It is a northern and western species.

134

Vervain Family

VERVAIN (*Verbena*)

147. Blue Vervain (*V. hastata*). Robust, usually clumped perennial of roads, pastures, and drier marshes. Stems, usually 2 to 4 feet tall, are square with opposite, tapering leaves that are coarsely toothed and often lobed. The small, deep blue flowers are in slender spikes, several of which top the individual stems. Occasionally the flowers are pink. Occurrence: Minnesota – throughout; general – eastern U.S. and adjacent Canada.

Both the common and botanical names mean "sacred bough," referring to ceremonial uses of a related species by Greeks and Romans.

147. Blue Vervain. Summer.

148. Hoary Vervain. Summer.

Vervain Family

148. Hoary Vervain (*V. stricta*). Erect, square-stemmed perennial, usually 1 to 3 feet tall, of pastures, roadsides, and open places. Leaves are oval, coarsely toothed, and covered with soft hairs. The flowers are usually mauve purple but sometimes rose or blue. They are in a cluster of elongate spikes at the top of the stem. Occurrence: Minnesota – mostly in the south ,and west; general – widely distributed in interior North America.

White Vervain (*V. urticifolia*) is a coarse, erect herb with tiny, white flowers on long, slender spikes. It grows in fields and waste places, sometimes near buildings and in shady places.

Mint Family

GERMANDER (*Teucrium*)

149. American Germander (*T. canadense*). Also called Wood Sage. Upright, little-branched perennial of moist, often somewhat shady places. The hairy, square stems, usually 1 to 2 feet tall, bear opposite, stalked leaves with blades that are rounded or tapering at the base. Flowers are 2-lipped, pink-purple, and in spirelike clusters. The top of the corolla is split, making an opening through which the stamens protrude. Occurrence: Minnesota — most common in southeastern third, but occasionally in the north; general — temperate North America.

149. American Germander. Summer.

150. Common Woundwort. Summer.

Mint Family

WOUNDWORT (*Stachys*)

150. Common Woundwort (*S. palustris*). Also called Hedge Nettle. Upright, usually unbranched perennial of wet, open places. The stem, usually 1 to 2 feet tall, is square and hairy. The opposite leaves are stalkless or nearly so, with blades abruptly narrowed at the base. The rose-purple flowers are in whorls on an elongate, tapering inflorescence. Each is 2-lipped, the upper lip covering the stamens. Occurrence: Minnesota — throughout; general — subarctic and temperate North America.

Woundwort was used by the Chippewa Indians as colic medicine.

Mint Family

SKULLCAP (*Scutellaria*)

151. Common Skullcap (*S. galericulata*). Slender perennial, usually 1 to 2 feet tall, of marshes, bogs, and shores. Stems are square and leaves opposite. The 2-lipped, blue flowers, about 1 inch long, are in the axils of the upper leaves. The calyx has a ridge or crest. Occurrence: Minnesota — throughout; general — much of subarctic and temperate North America.

Flowers of the **Mad-dog Skullcap** (*S. lateriflora*) are smaller and in loose clusters in the axils of the oval, pointed leaves. It is a common plant of moist places and once had a considerable, but unwarranted, reputation for treatment of hydrophobia.

151. Common Skullcap. Summer.

152. Fragrant Giant Hyssop. Summer.

Mint Family

GIANT HYSSOP (*Agastache*)

152. Fragrant Giant Hyssop (*A. foeniculum*). One of the most ornamental of our native mints. It is a perennial, commonly 2 to 4 feet tall, with dense, often interrupted, spikes of bright blue flowers. The leaves are toothed, opposite, and white beneath. They have an anise or licorice odor when crushed. Occurrence: Minnesota — throughout in dry, open, or semishady places. Often along roads; general — central and western North America.

153. Ground Ivy. Spring; summer.

154. Heal-all. Spring; summer.

Mint Family

GROUND IVY (*Glechoma*)

153. Ground Ivy (*G. hederacea*). Also called Creeping Charlie. Low, strongly scented perennial with slender, creeping stems. They are square and root at the nodes. In spring short, leafy, upright stems are produced on which are blue, 2-lipped flowers. Leaves are opposite and have wide, coarsely toothed blades. Occurrence: Minnesota — throughout in shady places, especially where the soil has been disturbed. Carpets the flood plains of many southeastern streams; general — a Eurasian species widely naturalized in North America.

Mint Family

HEAL-ALL (*Prunella*)

154. Heal-all (*P. vulgaris*). Also

138

called All-heal and Self-heal. Perennial, usually less than a foot tall, of moist, open, semishady places. Often grows in patches. Leaves are opposite and the stem square. The purple-blue flowers are in a short, thick spike which also contains broad, pointed, green or purplish bracts. Heal-all, as its name implies, was once used in folk medicine. The herbage is bitter and has little odor. Occurrence: Minnesota — widely distributed in moist, often shady places; general — subarctic to temperate North America. Also in Eurasia.

Mint Family

FALSE DRAGONHEAD
(*Physostegia*)

155. False Dragonhead (*P. virginiana*). Erect perennial, usually 2 to 3 feet tall, of marshes, moist, open woods, and stream banks. Stems and elongate, opposite leaves are smooth and without hairs. The showy, rosy-pink flowers are about an inch long and in spirelike, often branched, clusters. When the flower is pushed into a new position it will remain there, giving the species the alternate name Obedient Plant, which is used in some seed catalogues. The plant is grown as a garden perennial. Occurrence: Minnesota — throughout, but most common on river bottoms and in open floodplain forests in the east; general — eastern temperate North America.

155. False Dragonhead. Summer.

MOTHERWORT (*Leonurus*)

156. Motherwort (*L. cardiaca*). Robust perennial, up to 4 feet tall, with square, erect, and usually clumped stems. The opposite leaves are lobed near the base, and the 2-lipped, pink flowers are in dense clusters in the leaf axils. The clustered sepals persist through the winter. In spring growth starts as a clump of lobed basal leaves. Motherwort is a native of eastern Asia and was originally cultivated as a medicinal herb. Occurrence: Minnesota — throughout in waste places, often in the dooryards and along paths; general — widely naturalized in North America.

Mint Family

WILD BERGAMOT (*Monarda*)

157. Wild Bergamot (*M. fistulosa*).

156. Motherwort. Summer.

157. Wild Bergamot. Summer.

Also called Horsemint. Clumped perennial, usually 1 to 2 feet tall, growing in dry, open or brushy places. Often common on roadsides. The erect, square stems and opposite leaves are usually hairy. The lavender flowers have 2 lips and are arranged in heads. Leaves and stems have a strong odor. Indians used this and related species to treat digestive and respiratory ailments. Occurrence: Minnesota — mostly in the south and west where it is a conspicuous, summer wild flower on dry prairies; general — temperate North America.

The odor of the leaves combines mint and citrus. Bergamot is a kind of orange.

Mint Family

MINT (*Mentha*)

158. Wild Mint (*M. arvensis*). Also called Field Mint and Canada Mint. Common perennial of wet places. The opposite, toothed leaves have a strong minty odor. Flowers are clustered in the axils of normal-sized stem leaves. They are small and white, pale pink, or pale blue. Stems are often reclining at the base, and the plant is commonly 1 to 2 feet tall. Occurrence: Minnesota — throughout; general — widely distributed in North America and in Eurasia.

Spearmint (*M. spicata*), which sometimes escapes from gardens, has clusters of flowers in the axils of the reduced upper leaves.

158. Wild Mint. Summer.

141

159. Virginia Ground Cherry. Summer.

Nightshade Family

GROUND CHERRY (*Physalis*)

159. Virginia Ground Cherry (*P. virginiana*). Low, branched perennial, usually less than a foot tall, of dry, open woods, meadows, and prairies. Leaves are alternate with elongate blades. The yellow flowers have 5 spreading petals that are united at the base and have a brown center. The spherical, edible fruit is enclosed in a loose, papery husk, the inflated calyx. Occurrence: Minnesota—mostly in the south and west; general — temperate North America.

Nightshade Family

NIGHTSHADE (*Solanum*)

160. Bittersweet Nightshade (*S. dulcamara*). Also called Bittersweet and Poison Nightshade. Sprawling or climbing perennial vine. The clustered flowers have backward-curved petals and a central yellow "beak" of stamens and the pistil. The bright red berries are eaten by birds but are doubtfully edible for humans. They contain an alkaloid, dulcamarin, which has had medicinal uses. The leaves, which may be lobed, have a sweet and then a bit-

160. Bittersweet Nightshade. Summer.

ter taste, hence the name. Occurrence: Minnesota – throughout in moist, brushy places; general – a Eurasian native now widely naturalized in North America.

Figwort Family

MONKEY-FLOWER (*Mimulus*)

161. Square-stemmed Monkey-flower (*M. ringens*). Erect perennial, usually 1 to 2 feet tall, of wet, open or brushy places. The 4-sided, bluntly angled stem bears opposite, toothed leaves. In the axils of the leaves are the conspicuous, blue flowers. They are stalked, 2-lipped, and about 1 inch long. *Mimulus* is Latin for "little buffoon" and refers to the "grin" that can be produced by squeezing the sides of the corolla. Occurrence: Minnesota – throughout; general – temperate eastern North America.

The **Yellow Monkey-flower** (*M. glabratus*) is a low, spreading plant of spring seepage areas and edges of streams. It often grows in shallow water. The flowers are like those of Square-stemmed Monkey-flower but are pale yellow and about ½ inch long.

Figwort Family

MULLEIN (*Verbascum*)

162. Common Mullein (*V. thapsus*). Also called Flannel Plant and Aaron's Rod. Robust biennial, usually 3 to 6 feet tall. During its first year it grows as a rosette of large, soft, hairy leaves and in its second year develops a stout, leafy stalk ending in one or more thick flower spikes. The pale yellow flowers open in the morning, last but a day, and are replaced the following day by others below them. The leaf hairs are

161. Square-stemmed Monkey-flower. Summer.

branched and treelike. Occurrence: a European plant widely distributed in dry, open places, especially where the soil has been disturbed.

The dry spikes, soaked in tallow, were used by the Romans for torches, and the velvety leaves served the ancient Greeks as lamp wicks.

162. Common Mullein. Summer.

143

TURTLEHEAD (*Chelone*)

163. Turtlehead (*C. glabra*). Robust perennial, 1 to 3 feet tall, of grassy and brushy marshes and along streams. The erect, bluntly angled stems are often clumped and end in spikes of white flowers that are 2-lipped and 1 to 1½ inches long. As its name implies, the shape of the flower suggests the head of a turtle. Leaves are opposite, elongate, and coarsely toothed. Occurrence: Minnesota — mostly in the east and north; general — temperate eastern North America.

Figwort Family

PENSTEMON (*Penstemon*)

164. Large-flowered Penstemon (*P. grandiflorus*). One of the most beautiful of prairie wild flowers. The pale purple, bell-shaped flowers, about 2 inches long, are in an elongate, spikelike cluster. The plant is perennial, usually 2 to 3 feet tall, and the bluish-green stem leaves are opposite, rather wide and without teeth. Occurrence: Minnesota — sandy prairies in central and west; general — central U.S. This and other penstemons are often called Beard-tongue because one of the 5 stamens has no anther and is hairy.

The **Slender Penstemon** (*P. gracilis*) has smaller, pale purple flowers, about ¾ inch long, is lower growing, and has narrow, toothed leaves. It is found in grassy places throughout much of Minnesota.

163. Turtlehead. Summer.

164. Large-flowered Penstemon. Summe

165. Foxglove Penstemon. Spring; summer.

166. Butter-and-eggs. Summer.

165. Foxglove Penstemon (*P. digitalis*). Has white, bell-shaped flowers, about an inch long, that are penciled inside with purple. The broad-based leaves taper to a point and are toothed. Except in the branched inflorescence, the stem is without hairs. Occurrence: Minnesota — rare, along eastern edge; general — eastern and central U.S.

The **White-flowered Penstemon** (*P. albidus*) is similar but has smaller, white flowers in a less spreading inflorescence and stems covered with minute hairs. It is a plant of prairies and plains, and in Minnesota is found mostly in the west.

Figwort Family

BUTTER-AND-EGGS (*Linaria*)

166. Butter-and-eggs (*L. vulgaris*). Also called Toadflax. Upright perennial, usually 1 to 2 feet tall, of roadsides, pastures, and waste places. It often grows in patches. The stem bears many narrow leaves and ends in a cluster of conspicuous, yellow flowers. The flower is 2-lipped and has a spur. An orange spot on the lower lip probably serves as a target for flying insects. Occurrence: a European species widely naturalized in Minnesota and elsewhere in North America.

It is quite ornamental and was planted in pioneer gardens.

CULVER'S ROOT (*Veronicastrum*)

167. Culver's Root (*V. virginicum*). Erect perennial of prairies and open woods. Usually 2 to 5 feet tall, it has elongate leaves in whorls of 3 to 6 and small, white flowers in tapering spikes. Each flower has 2 stamens that are longer than the petals. Occurrence: Minnesota — throughout, but most common on prairies in the south and west; general — temperate eastern North America.

The root is somewhat poisonous and was used medicinally by Indian and pioneer doctors. One of the latter was a Dr. Culver for whom the plant is named.

Figwort Family

GERARDIA (*Gerardia*)

168. Rough Gerardia (*G. aspera*). A slender, branched annual of moist prairies, often growing among grasses. The rosy-pink, bell-shaped flowers are about 1 inch long and on ascending stalks. The stems and narrow leaves are rough with short hairs. Occurrence: Minnesota — prairies in the west and south; general — temperate central North America.

The **Small-flowered Gerardia** (*G. paupercula*) has similar but smaller flowers and smooth leaves and stems. It grows in damp meadows, marshes, and seepage areas.

The generic name commemorates John Gerarde (1545-1612), English botanist and herbalist.

167. Culver's Root. Summer.

168. Rough Gerardia. Summer.

147

169. Common Lousewort. Summer.

Figwort Family

LOUSEWORT (*Pedicularis*)

169. Common Lousewort (*P. canadensis*). Also called Wood Betony. Low, hairy perennial, usually 6 to 12 inches tall, of dry meadows,

170. Indian Paint Brush. Summer.

prairies, and upland woods. The elongate leaves have many side lobes. Flowers are 2-lipped, commonly yellow, and in dense clusters. Occurrence: Minnesota — mostly in the south and west; general — temperate eastern North America.

The **Swamp Lousewort** (*P. lanceolata*) is similar but taller and with white or nearly white flowers. It grows in wet, open places.

Both the common and generic names refer to the ancient belief that cattle become lousy by feeding on lousewort.

Figwort Family

INDIAN PAINT BRUSH (*Castilleja*)

170. Indian Paint Brush (*C. coccinea*). Also called Painted Cup. Among the brightest of summer wild flowers. It is an annual with erect stems, usually 1 to 2 feet tall. The stem is topped with a cluster of bright red or, less commonly, yellow leaves which might be mistaken for petals. Among these colored leaves are the inconspicuous, yellowish, 2-lipped flowers. The green stem leaves have narrow, pointed lobes. Indian Paint Brush is semiparasitic, its roots tapping those of other plants. Occurrence: Minnesota — throughout, except in the southwest and extreme west; general — temperate eastern North America.

The rarer **Downy Painted Cup** (*C. sessiliflora*) is a prairie plant, usually less than a foot tall. Its leaves are covered with soft, gray hairs.

Bladderwort Family

BLADDERWORT (*Utricularia*)

171. Greater Bladderwort (*U. vulgaris*). A remarkable, carnivorous aquatic plant of quiet, shallow waters. The elongate stems float just beneath the water surface and have much divided, submerged leaves on which are tiny bladderlike traps that capture and digest minute aquatic animals. In summer, short, leafless stems emerge from the water. Each bears 2-lipped, yellow flowers, about 1 inch long. The flower has a short spur at its base. Occurrence: Minnesota — throughout in shallow, undisturbed waters; general — circumpolar, in North America from subarctic to southern U.S. and Mexico.

Madder Family

HOUSTONIA (*Houstonia*)

172. Long-leaved Houstonia (*H. longifolia*). Low, often clumped perennial of dry, open places. Usually 4 to 8 inches tall. The flowers have 4 white or pale purple petals and are in small, spreading clusters. Stems are erect with elongate, opposite leaves that are without teeth. Oc-

currence: Minnesota — widespread, usually in undisturbed, open, sandy and rocky places; general — eastern U.S. and adjacent Canada.

171. Greater Bladderwort. Summer.

172. Long-leaved Houstonia. Spring; summer.

173. Northern Bedstraw. Spring; summer.

Madder Family

BEDSTRAW (*Galium*)

173. Northern Bedstraw (*G. boreale*). Common, white wild flower of late spring. It is usually 1 to 2 feet tall and grows in well-drained, open places. The small, 4-petaled flowers are in a dense cluster at the top of the square stem. Leaves are elongate, without teeth, and in whorls of 4. The flowers are sweet-scented. Occurrence: Minnesota — throughout on prairies and brushy places, often common along roads; general — temperate North America and also in Eurasia.

There are several other species of bedstraw in Minnesota. All have whorled leaves, square stems, and small, 4-petaled, white flowers. **Cleavers** (*G. aparine*) is a common sprawling plant of damp woods and brushy places. It clings to clothing by hooklike hairs on the stem angles.

174. Twin-flower. Summer.

TWIN-FLOWER (*Linnaea*)

174. Twin-flower (*L. borealis*). Low, trailing perennial of cool, moist woods and bogs. The nodding, pink flowers are bell-shaped, about ½ inch long, and in pairs at the top of slender stalks. Leaves are evergreen and opposite on the stems. Occurrence: Minnesota — north and east-central, mostly in coniferous forests and muskegs; general — circumpolar, from subarctic south to temperate regions.

Linnaea commemorates Carl Linnaeus (1707-1778), the father of modern plant classification. This plant was his favorite wild flower.

Valerian Family

VALERIAN (*Valeriana*)

175. Common Valerian (*V. officinalis*). Perennial of brushy places and swamps. It is usually 2 to 3 feet tall and has pinnately compound leaves and fibrous roots. The small, white or pinkish flowers are in compact clusters at the top of the stem. They are followed by seedlike fruits ending in feathery bristles. Occurrence: A native of Eurasia, it has escaped from old gardens and become naturalized here and there. In Minnesota it is occasional in the Twin Cities area and fairly common in Duluth.

The native *V. edulis*, a perennial with thick roots and a cluster of elongate basal leaves, is found in southern Minnesota swamps.

Valerian root contains several strong-smelling substances, including valeric acid. The dried root has been used medicinally since ancient times. Cats are attracted by its odor.

175. Common Valerian. Summer.

176. Wild Cucumber. Summer.

176a. Wild Cucumber in fruit. Autumn.

Gourd Family

WILD CUCUMBER (*Echinocystis*)

176. Wild Cucumber (*E. lobata*). Also called Balsam Apple. Annual vine with square stems, deeply lobed leaves, and branched tendrils. The showy male flowers are white and in erect clusters, and the less evident female flowers are in the leaf axils. The ovoid fruits, about 2 inches long, are prickly. Eventually 4 large, black seeds are released through a hole in the lower end of the fruit, leaving behind the papery shells. Within is a 2-legged network of vascular tissue known to children as "lace pants." Occurrence: Minnesota — common in moist, brushy places; general — temperate eastern North America.

The **Bur** or **Star Cucumber** (*Sicyos angulatus*) is a fairly common herbaceous vine of moist, shady places. It has hairy stems, shallowly lobed leaves, tendrils, and burlike clusters of 1-seeded fruits.

Bellflower Family

BELLFLOWER (*Campanula*)

177. Harebell (*C. rotundifolia*). Also called Bluebell and Bluebells of Scotland. Graceful and common perennial of dry prairies, roadsides, open woods, and rocky places. The clumped, slender stems range in height from a few inches to more than a foot. Stem leaves are elongate and pointed, and the bell-shaped, blue flowers are in a loose cluster. Basal leaves are rounded or bluntly heart-shaped, hence the specific name. As in other members of this genus, the juice is milky. Occurrence: Minnesota — throughout, except in the extreme south and southwest; general — arctic circumpolar, south in North America to temperate U.S.

Harebell is easily cultured in gardens and does well in rockeries.

177. Harebell. Summer.

178. European Bellflower. Summer.

179. American Bellflower. Summer.

178. European Bellflower (*C. rapunculoides*). Perennial of roadsides and waste places, often near old gardens and dooryards. It has stiff, erect stems, 1 to 3 feet tall, ending in elongate, 1-sided clusters of pale purple, bell-shaped flowers. They are nodding and about 1 inch long. The plants spread by rootstalks and often form patches. Occurrence: a European plant once grown in gardens and now widely naturalized in Minnesota and elsewhere in North America.

The **Clustered Bellflower** (*C. glomerata*), also from Europe, is well established along roads near Duluth. It is an erect perennial, usually 1 to 2 feet tall, with the stem ending in a compact cluster of bluish-purple flowers.

Bellflower Family

179. American Bellflower (*C. americana*). Erect annual or biennial, usually 2 to 4 feet tall. The blue flowers are in a leafy spike. Each flower is about 1 inch wide with 5 spreading petals joined at the base. There is a long, curved style in the center. Leaves are toothed and taper toward both ends. Occurrence: Minnesota — mostly in the southern one-third in moist woods and along shady streams; general — temperate eastern North America.

Lobelia Family

LOBELIA (*Lobelia*)

180. Cardinal Flower (*L. cardinalis*). Perennial of damp, open or somewhat shady places. Commonly 2 to 3 feet tall. The intense red flowers are in an elongate cluster. Each is

180. Cardinal Flower. Summer.

about 1 inch across and has 3 spreading lower petals and 2 upright petals. The petals are united into a tube toward their base. Occasionally plants have white or rose flowers. Juice is milky and acrid. Occurrence: Minnesota — mostly in the east as far north as Pine County, especially along streams; general — temperate eastern North America.

Cardinal Flower has long been grown in gardens. It requires a moist spot and will tolerate some shade.

181. Great Blue Lobelia. Summer; autumn.

182. Kalm's Lobelia. Summer.

Lobelia Family

181. Great Blue Lobelia (*L. siphilitica*). Erect perennial, usually 1 to 2 feet tall, of wet places. The flowers resemble those of the Cardinal Flower but are blue or occasionally white. Occurrence: Minnesota — throughout, often in swamps and along streams and ditches; general — temperate eastern North America.

This species has sometimes been called Hi-belia to contrast it, perhaps facetiously, with lower-growing, blue-flowered kinds. It, and several other members of the genus, contain a toxic compound, lobeline. *Lobelia* honors Matthias de l'Obel (1538-1616), a Flemish botanist.

Lobelia Family

182. Kalm's Lobelia (*L. kalmii*). Also called Northern Lobelia. A beautiful low-growing lobelia, usually less than 1 foot tall. The small, pale blue flowers are about ½ inch across, have white centers, and are each on a slender stalk. Occurrence: Minnesota — occasional, in moist, open places, except in extreme south; general — subarctic North America south to northern U.S.

The **Pale-spike Lobelia** (*L. spicata*) is similar but has a long inflorescence of small, uniformly blue flowers on short stalks. It is a plant of dry prairies and meadows and is usually 1 to 2 feet tall.

Composite Family

SUNFLOWER (*Helianthus*)

183. Common Sunflower (*H. annuus*). Robust, usually branched annual of dry, open places. Commonly 2 to 5 feet tall with flower heads 3 to 6 inches across. The center or the head (disk) is brown or purple. Leaves are coarsely toothed and often heart-shaped. Occurrence: Minnesota — throughout, often on disturbed soil along roads; general — temperate North America but most common in the west. This plant is the ancestor of the cultivated sunflower.

The **Stiff Sunflower** (*H. laetiflorus*) also has heads with dark disks. It is a prairie perennial, often growing on sandy soils. Stems are slender and wiry and usually 2 to 4 feet tall. The opposite leaves are rough and mostly 3-nerved.

Composite Family

184. Woodland Sunflower (*H. divaricatus*). Perennial, usually 2 to 4 feet tall, of open woods and woodland edges. Flower heads have yellow disks and are mostly at the ends of the forked stems. Leaves are opposite, widest near the base, and stalkless or nearly so. Occurrence: Minnesota — mostly in the hardwood

183. Common Sunflower. Summer; autumn.

forest areas of the south; general — temperate eastern North America.

This species often grows in shady dooryards.

184. Woodland Sunflower. Summer; autumn.

185. Jerusalem Artichoke. Summer; autumn.

186. Maximilian's Sunflower. Summer; autumn.

Composite Family

185. Jerusalem Artichoke (*H. tuberosus*). Robust perennial sunflower, often 5 to 8 feet tall. The heads have yellow disks and the leaf blades are less than 3 times as long as broad. Gnarled tubers are produced at the base of the stem. They were eaten by Indians and are still raised for food. The tubers are of value for special diets since they contain inulin, not starch. Occurrence: Minnesota — throughout on upland soils but most common in the south and west; general — temperate eastern North America west to the Rocky Mountains.

Two other perennial sunflowers are similar but have narrow leaves. Both thrive in wet places. The **Giant Sunflower** (*H. giganteus*) is most common in the north. Stems are hairy below the inflorescence and the leaves usually have few teeth. **Sawtooth Sunflower** (*H. grosseserratus*), which is most common in the south, has hairless stems and usually coarsely toothed leaves.

Composite Family

186. Maximilian's Sunflower (*H. maximiliani*). A prairie perennial, usually 3 to 5 feet tall. The elongate, keeled, and arching leaves are rough with short hairs. The disk of the flower head is yellow. This sunflower is named after Prince Maximilian of Wied, Germany, who early in the last century traveled the plains with artist Carl Bodmer, known for his paintings of Indians and western scenery. Occurrence: prairies and plains of Minnesota and central North America, often on sandy soil.

158

187. Ox-eye. Spring; summer.

Composite Family

OX-EYE (*Heliopsis*)

187. Ox-eye (*H. helianthoides*). Perennial, usually 1 to 3 feet tall, with stiff, erect stems, sunflowerlike heads, and opposite leaves that have wide, toothed blades. Heads are usually about 2 inches across and have raised centers. The yellow rays remain attached to the head after withering. Ox-eye begins to bloom in late spring and continues throughout most of the summer. Occurrence: Minnesota — throughout on prairies, roadsides, and in open woods; general—much of temperate North America.

There are double cultivars that resemble a yellow zinnia.

Composite Family

CONEFLOWER (*Rudbeckia*)

188. Brown-eyed Susan (*R. hirta*). A common, bright, summer wild flower of roadsides and fields. The slender, erect stems are usually 1 to 2 feet tall. They end in flower heads that have raised, rounded centers that are purplish-brown and surrounded by yellow rays. Occasionally the rays are brown at the base. Leaves are elongate, without lobes, and frequently have 3 nerves. Occurrence: Minnesota — throughout, often on sandy soil; general — temperate eastern North America.

188. Brown-eyed Susan. Summer.

189. Wild Golden Glow. Summer.

190. Purple Coneflower. Summer.

189. Wild Golden Glow (*R. laciniata*). Also called Green-headed Coneflower. A robust and usually clumped perennial, often 5 to, 8 feet tall, with large lower leaves that are lobed or divided. Flower heads are 2 to 3 inches across. They have drooping, yellow rays and raised, greenish centers. Occurrence: Minnesota — most common in the southeast in moist, often brushy places; general — temperate eastern North America.

A double variety, the **Garden Golden Glow**, is sometimes established along roads near old gardens and dwellings. This is the only instance we know of in which the name of the wild plant is derived from the garden variety.

PURPLE CONEFLOWER
(*Echinacea*)

190. Purple Coneflower (*E. angustifolia*). A perennial, usually 1 to 2 feet tall, of dry prairies. Flower heads have purple rays and a raised, spiny center. The slender stem and 3-nerved leaves are covered with coarse hairs. Occurrence: Minnesota — prairies, mostly in the west; general — temperate western North America.

According to Lycurgus Moyer, pioneer Minnesota jurist and botanist, early travelers on the prairie called it Thirst Plant because the roots had a "salty, peppery taste." When they were chewed the flow of saliva was increased, relieving the traveler's thirst when good drinking water was not to be had.

160

Composite Family

PRAIRIE CONEFLOWER
(*Ratibida*)

191. Gray-headed Coneflower (*R. pinnata*). Perennial of open places and edges of woods. The showy flower heads have drooping, yellow rays and raised, grayish centers that are shorter than the rays. Both the erect stems, commonly 1 to 3 feet tall, and the divided leaves are covered with short, gray hairs. Occurrence: Minnesota — mostly in the south where it is often common along roads and railways; general — temperate eastern North America.

The **Long-headed Coneflower** (*R. columnifera*) is similar, but the flower heads have a dark, columnar center longer than the rays. Rays are usually yellow but may be partly or wholly purple. A plant of western, dry prairies and plains; in Minnesota in the south and west.

191. Gray-headed Coneflower. Summer.

Composite Family

TICKSEED (*Coreopsis*)

192. Stiff Tickseed (*C. palmata*). Early summer wild flower of open places. The stiff, erect stems, usually 1 to 2 feet tall, end in flower heads about 1½ inches across. They have 6 to 10 yellow rays, each ending in 3 blunt teeth. Leaves are opposite and have 3 elongate lobes. The stems rise from running rootstalks and often are in patches. Occurrence: Minnesota — well-drained prairies and open woods in the south, often common along railways; general — central North America from Manitoba to Texas.

192. Stiff Tickseed. Early summer.

Composite Family
BEGGAR'S-TICKS (*Bidens*)

193. Nodding Beggar's-ticks (*B. cernua*). Also called Bur Marigold and Stick-tight. Annual, usually 1 to 2 feet tall, of wet places such as marshes and pond margins. The small, sunflowerlike heads have 6 to 8 yellow rays and are nodding when in fruit. Bases of the opposite leaves are often joined. The elongate, flat fruits end in 2 to 4 barbed awns which stick tightly to clothing and fur. Occurrence: widespread in Minnesota, temperate North America, and Eurasia.

Composite Family
ROSINWEED (*Silphium*)

194. Cup Plant (*S. perfoliatum*). Stout perennial, usually 3 to 6 feet tall, with sunflowerlike heads up to 4 inches across. Stems are square, and the wide, opposite leaves are united at the base to form a "cup." The heads are arranged in a spreading cluster and have 20 to 30 yellow rays. Occurrence: Minnesota — on moist, fertile soils, especially in river valleys in the south, but not common; general — temperate eastern North America.

The flower heads of *Silphium* have fertile, seed-producing ray flowers and sterile disk flowers. In sunflowers (*Helianthus*) the opposite is true.

Composite Family

195. Compass Plant (*S. laciniatum*). Also called Rosinweed. Among the tallest of our nonwoody plants, often reaching a height of 6 to 8 feet. This typical prairie perennial has

193. Nodding Beggar's-ticks. Autumn.

194. Cup Plant. Summer; autumn.

162

flower heads with yellow rays much like those of sunflowers. They are usually 3 to 4 inches across. The large, hairy leaves are deeply cut and divided. Occurrence: Minnesota — mostly in the south on undisturbed prairie remnants; general — eastern U.S. but now rare.

When Compass Plant grows in dry, open places, the lower leaves often stand on edge and are oriented in a north-south direction, hence its name. Resinous material collects where a stem is broken. This was chewed by pioneer children. The plant is highly palatable to cattle and easily destroyed by grazing.

Composite Family

SNEEZEWEED (*Helenium*)

196. Sneezeweed (*H. autumnale*). Perennial, usually 2 to 4 feet tall, with elongate leaves, the bases of which extend down the stem as flanges or wings. The numerous flower heads have raised, nearly globular centers and wedge-shaped, yellow rays which end in 3 coarse teeth. Often the stems are clumped. Occurrence: widespread in moist, open places in Minnesota and elsewhere in temperate North America. It often grows along streams.

The flowers release a volatile oil that has insecticidal properties. Menomini Indians used the dried flower heads to promote sneezing to loosen a head cold. There are garden cultivars, called Helen's Flower, with yellow to brick red flowers.

195. Compass Plant. Summer, autumn.

196. Sneezeweed. Summer; autumn.

163

or rosy flower heads are grown in gardens and sometimes occur in the wild. Occurrence: a European plant widely naturalized along roads and in old fields and pastures. In Europe it was once used for flavoring beer.

The native **Western** or **Woolly Yarrow** (*A. lanulosa*) is similar but has an abundance of woolly hairs on the stem. Leaf divisions stand in several planes rather than lying nearly flat. It is common throughout Minnesota on prairies and in open woods. Sometimes considered a variant (subspecies) of the Common Yarrow.

Composite Family

OX-EYE DAISY (*Chrysanthemum*)

198. Ox-eye Daisy (*C. leucanthemum*). The common, white daisy of roadsides and old pastures. This perennial, a native of Europe, spreads by rootstalks and often grows in patches. Each slender, unbranched stem, usually 1 to 2 feet tall, ends in a flower head with a yellow center and many white rays, up to an inch long. Leaves are elongate and variously toothed and lobed. Occurrence: Minnesota — widespread but most common in the northeastern third; general — throughout temperate North America.

The number of rays per head varies considerably, giving rise to the petal-plucking children's game of "loves me, loves me not." Marie-Victorin, the famous French-Canadian botanist, noted that counting the rays on a large number of heads provides a useful classroom ap-

197. Common Yarrow. Summer.

Composite Family

YARROW (*Achillea*)

197. Common Yarrow (*A. millefolium*). Erect, often clumped perennial with flat clusters of small, white flower heads. The elongate leaves are strongly scented, nearly flat, and much divided. Plants with pink

164

198. Ox-eye Daisy. Summer.

proach to the statistics of biological variation.

Composite Family

TANSY (*Tanacetum*)

199. Tansy (*T. vulgare*). A European perennial once grown as a flavoring and medicinal plant. The stems, usually 2 to 4 feet tall and often in clumps or patches, are topped by flat clusters of rayless, yellow flower heads. The elongate, much divided leaves are strongly scented and bitter. Tansy was once used in cooking, cheese making, and as a tonic tea. However, it can be poisonous if too much is used. Occurrence: widely naturalized in Minnesota and elsewhere in temperate North America, especially along roads and in old fields and dooryards.

199. Tansy. Summer.

200. Mayweed. Summer.

Composite Family

CHAMOMILE
(*Anthemis* and *Matricaria*)

200. Mayweed (*A. cotula*). Also called Dog Fennel and Dog Chamomile. Low, strongly scented annual with flower heads having raised, conical centers and white rays. Leaves are much cut and divided. Usually it is less than 2 feet tall. Occurrence: a weedy Eurasian species widely distributed on fertile, disturbed soils, such as barnyards, turkey pastures, and road shoulders along which manure has been hauled.

Under the name Feverweed, this plant went west with the pioneers. An Ozark tale tells of Johnny Appleseed planting it in new settlements after his wife and child had died of "chills."

Scentless Chamomile (*M. mariti-ma*) is similar but often taller and with finely cut leaves that are nearly odorless. It also is of European origin and in Minnesota is found in the north, especially along Lake Superior.

Composite Family

201. Pineapple-weed (*M. matricarioides*). Low, weedy annual, usually less than 6 inches tall. The small flower heads are greenish and without rays. Leaves are much divided and when crushed have a pineapple odor. Patches of Pineapple-weed also give off this odor after a rain. Occurrence: a native of the western U.S., it has become naturalized in eastern North America and Europe. In Minnesota it often grows in dooryards and along driveways.

Pineapple-weed thrives in areas grazed by geese and ducks such as

166

around Silver Lake, Rochester, Minnesota. We have also seen it growing in goose pens in northern England.

Composite Family

SAGE AND WORMWOOD
(*Artemisia*)

202. Prairie Sage (*A. ludoviciana*). Erect perennial, usually 1 to 2 feet tall, with leaves covered on both sides with soft, white hairs. The leaves are usually without teeth and have an aromatic, sage-brush odor when crushed. The small, grayish flower heads are in an elongate, pyramidal cluster. Occurrence: Minnesota — prairies and pastures in the south and west, often growing in patches; general — western North America.

The **Saw-tooth Prairie Sage** (*A. serrata*) is similar but has coarsely toothed leaves that are green above and white beneath. It is a midwestern species growing in open, grassy places, usually on moister sites than the Prairie Sage.

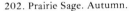

202. Prairie Sage. Autumn.

201. Pineapple-weed. Summer.

Composite Family

203. Common Wormwood (*A. absinthium*). Also called Absinth and Mugwort. Robust perennial, usually 1 to 3 feet tall, with much divided leaves that are very aromatic and gray with soft, silky hairs. The small, gray flower heads are in an elongate, somewhat leafy cluster. Occurrence: Minnesota — dry fields, roadsides, and waste places. It thrives in overgrazed pastures; general — a European species that is widely naturalized in temperate North America. In Europe it was once an ingredient in the habit-forming liqueur absinthe, a use now outlawed.

Composite Family

RAGWORT (*Senecio*)

204. Prairie Ragwort (*S. plattensis*). Prairie perennial, usually 1 to 2 feet tall, with a spreading cluster of small flower heads, each having yellow rays and a cuplike involucre composed of a single row of narrow, green bracts. The basal leaves are stalked and toothed, and the narrower stem leaves are often irregularly toothed and lobed. Stems and leaves are woolly with soft, white hairs. Occurrence: Minnesota — dry prairies, mostly in the south and west; general — central and western temperate North America.

Balsam Ragwort (*S. pauperculus*) is a similar but less woolly plant of northern woods and sandy places. **Golden Ragwort** (*S. aureus*) grows on wet soil. Its flowers are similar to those of Prairie Ragwort, but the basal leaves are heart-shaped, toothed, and have a marked balsamic odor when crushed.

203. Common Wormwood. Summer.

204. Prairie Ragwort. Late spring; summer.

Composite Family

GOLDEN ASTER (*Chrysopsis*)

205. Golden Aster (*C. villosa*). Branched, often clumped and bushy perennial, usually 1 to 2 feet tall, of dry, open places. The flower heads are about 1 inch across and have yellow rays. Leaves and stems are hairy. Occurrence: Minnesota — prairies and brushy places, often on sand, most common in the west and central; general — upper Midwest and Great Plains.

Composite Family

GUM PLANT (*Grindelia*)

206. Gum Plant (*G. squarrosa*). Also called Gum-weed. Glabrous biennial or perennial of open' places and coarse soils. The erect, often clumped stems are commonly 1 to 3 feet tall and the yellow-rayed flower heads are about 1 inch across. The narrow involucre bracts beneath the rays are backward-curved and sticky with a resinous, odorous gum. Leaves are elongate and usually toothed. Occurrence: widely distributed, especially along roads and railways in Minnesota and elsewhere in North America.

205. Golden Aster. Summer; autumn.

206. Gum Plant. Summer; autumn.

207. Stiff Goldenrod. Summer; autumn.
208. Grass-leaved Goldenrod. Summer; autumn.

209. Zigzag Goldenrod. Summer, autumn.

Composite Family

GOLDENROD (*Solidago*)

207. Stiff Goldenrod (*S. rigida*). Flower heads are in a wide, flat or somewhat rounded cluster that is several inches across. Stems are often clumped and commonly 2 to 4 feet tall. The oval to oblong stem leaves and the stalked basal leaves are rough with short, stiff hairs. Occurrence: Minnesota — prairies and roadsides, especially in the south and west; general — temperate North America.

This and the following species are perennials that bloom in late summer and autumn. All have small heads of yellow flowers and alternate stem leaves.

Composite Family

208. Grass-leaved Goldenrod (*S. graminifolia*). Flower heads are in a loose, flattish cluster. The stems, usually 1 to 2 feet tall, are branched upward and have elongate, narrow leaves, usually with 3 parallel veins (nerves). Occurrence: Minnesota — open and brushy places, often on sandy soil; general — temperate North America.

Composite Family

209. Zigzag Goldenrod (*S. flexicaulis*). Woodland goldenrod with erect, somewhat zigzag stems. The pointed, oval leaves are coarsely toothed. Flower heads are in small, often stalked clusters at the base of the upper leaves. Occurrence: Minnesota — woods and woodland edges, especially in hardwood forest areas; general — temperate eastern North America.

170

210. Showy Goldenrod. Summer; autumn.

Composite Family

210. Showy Goldenrod (*S. speciosa*). Flower heads in a blunt, plumelike cluster that has ascending (not arching) side branches. Stems are usually clumped, 1 to 3 feet tall, and the herbage is nearly hairless. One of the most beautiful goldenrods. Occurrence: Minnesota — prairies and open woods, especially in the south and west, often on sandy soil; general — eastern and central U.S.

The **Hairy Goldenrod** (*S. hispida*) also has a blunt inflorescence with ascending branches. However, the inflorescence is narrow. Flower heads are usually orange-yellow, and the herbage is hairy. It grows in dry, sandy and rocky places throughout Minnesota.

211. Canada Goldenrod. Summer; autumn.

Composite Family

211. Canada Goldenrod (*S. canadensis*). Common roadside and pasture goldenrod. Its plumes of yellow flower heads nod at the tip and have arching side branches. Stems are commonly 2 to 4 feet tall and grow in clumps or patches. The upper leafy part of the stem is hairy. The leaves decrease gradually in size upward on the stem, are coarsely toothed, and have 3 main veins (nerves). Occurrence: Minnesota—throughout; general—temperate North America.

Late Goldenrod (*S. gigantea*) is similar but more robust, often as tall as 5 or 6 feet. Stems are hairless and usually shiny and reddish. It is most common in moist, open places.

Both species often have a rounded swelling (gall) on the stem, caused by an insect. The fly grub they contain is used for winter fishing bait.

Composite Family

212. Gray Goldenrod (*S. nemoralis*). Low, slender goldenrod, usually not taller than 2 feet, of prairies and dry roadsides. It has ashy gray herbage and basal leaves markedly larger than the stem leaves. The cluster of flower heads nods and is somewhat 1-sided. Occurrence: Common on dry, open places in Minnesota and elsewhere in temperate western North America.

Composite Family

213. Missouri Goldenrod (*S. missouriensis*). Low-growing and early, flowering goldenrod of prairies. It is usually 1 to 2 feet tall. Stem leaves are narrow, toothed, and firmly erect. The herbage, including the bracts of the flower heads, is smooth and hairless. Leaves are markedly 3-nerved. The large basal leaves are usually gone at the time of flowering. Occurrence: Minnesota — prairies in south and west; general — typical goldenrod of the Great Plains.

The **Early Goldenrod** (*S. juncea*) is quite similar but is a plant of northern forest openings and roadsides, especially on sandy soil. Often blossoms in July. The inflorescence is nodding and about as wide as long. Usually there is a tuft of large, rather soft basal leaves that are somewhat 3-nerved.

212. Gray Goldenrod. Summer; early autumn.

213. Missouri Goldenrod. Summer; early autumn.

173

214. Large-leaved Aster. Autumn.

215. Lindley's Aster. Late summer; autumn.

Composite Family

ASTER (*Aster*)

214. Large-leaved Aster (*A. macrophyllus*). A common plant of northern forests, the heart-shaped basal leaves often covering the forest floor. Leaves are coarsely toothed and rough to touch. The flowering stems, mostly 1 to 2 feet tall, are topped by a spreading cluster of flower heads, each with 9 to 20 pale purple rays. Occurrence: Minnesota — upland forests, especially in the north; general — temperate eastern North America.

This and the following species of *Aster* are perennials blooming in late summer and autumn. The flower heads have narrow rays which are white, blue, or purple. Stem leaves are alternate and the crushed herbage often has a resinous odor.

Aster is Latin for "star."

Composite Family

215. Lindley's Aster (*A. ciliolatus*). Common, tall aster of upland forest areas and roadsides, especially in the north. It is usually 2 to 4 feet tall. The lower leaves are elongate, somewhat heart-shaped, and hairless. Margins of lower leaves are toothed. The flower heads, arranged in an elongate, spreading cluster, have 10 to 20 blue or purplish rays. Occurrence: Minnesota — mostly in the north; general — northern U.S. and adjacent Canada.

216. Azure Aster. Late summer; autumn.

Composite Family

216. Azure Aster (*A. azureus*). A prairie aster, quite similar to the preceding but with lower leaves that have few or no teeth. It is usually 1 to 2 feet tall. Occurrence: Minnesota — prairies, especially in the southeast and central; general — eastern U.S.

The seedlike fruits of this and other asters are tipped with a tuft of hairs by which they are wind-transported.

175

217. Blue Wood Aster. Late summer; autumn.

Composite Family

217. Blue Wood Aster (*A. cordifolius*). Woodland aster with small, blue, lavender, or white flower heads and coarsely toothed, heart-shaped leaves. It is usually 1 to 3 feet tall. Stems are much branched and commonly in clumps. Occurrence: Minnesota — wooded areas, mostly in the south and southeast. It frequently invades shady dooryards and gardens; general — eastern U.S.

Composite Family

218. New England Aster (*A. novae-angliae*). Robust, hairy aster with deep purple, or sometimes rosy, flower heads that are 1 to 1½ inch-

218. New England Aster. Autumn.

es across and have more than 30 narrow rays. Stems, often as tall as 4 feet, are usually clumped and much branched. Bases of the oblong stem leaves clasp the stem. Occurrence: Minnesota — common in moist, open places except in the northeast; general—temperate eastern and central North America.

This aster is often grown as a garden perennial. There is also a white variety.

Composite Family

219. Red-stalked Aster (*A. puniceus*). Stout aster of open and brushy, wet places. The flower heads, which are 1 to 1½ inches across, have more than 30 pale blue or purplish rays. The stem, commonly 3 to 5 feet tall, is often reddish, has scattered bristly hairs, and clasping leaves that are usually toothed. Occurrence: Minnesota — throughout in wet places except in the southwest; general — eastern U.S.

Composite Family

220. Smooth Aster (*A. laevis*). A beautiful aster of open or brushy places such as prairie swales and roadsides. It is usually 2 to 4 feet tall and has hairless leaves that clasp the stem. Basal leaves, if present, are not heart-shaped. The flowers are about 1 inch across with 15 to 25 bright blue or blue-purple rays. Occurrence: Minnesota — throughout, except in the northeast; general — temperate North America.

Smooth Aster is sometimes grown in gardens.

177

219. Red-stalked Aster. Autumn.

220. Smooth Aster. Summer; autumn.

221. Aromatic Aster. Autumn.

Composite Family

221. Aromatic Aster (*A. oblongifo-lius*). Low, much-branched aster of dry prairies. It is usually less than 2 feet tall. Flower heads have rosy-purple rays and beneath these are curved, spreading bracts which are sticky with aromatic hairs. Stems are brittle, and the oblong, pointed leaves are without stalks. Occurrence: Minnesota — dry prairies and open rocky places, mostly in the south; general — eastern and central U.S.

Composite Family

222. Silky Aster (*A. sericeus*). Low, branched aster of dry, open places. It is usually 1 to 2 feet tall and has small, pointed leaves covered with silky hairs on both sides. The flower heads have rosy-purple rays. Occurrence: Minnesota — south and west on dry prairies; general — temperate central North America.

Composite Family

223. Panicled Aster (*A. simplex*). A common, tall, white aster of drier, open marshes. It is usually 2 to 4 feet tall. The herbage is hairless or nearly so, and flower heads are about ¾ inch wide with 20 or more white rays. The stem is much branched toward the top. Occurrence: Minnesota — throughout; general — eastern and central U.S. and adjacent Canada.

222. Silky Aster. Autumn.

223. Panicled Aster. Autumn.

224. Upland White Aster. Summer; autumn.

225. Flat-top White Aster. Autumn.

Composite Family

224. Upland White Aster (*A. ptarmicoides*). Low, white aster, commonly with clumped stems less than 1½ feet tall. Flower heads are about 1 inch across. It is the only species having heads with both white rays and white centers. Occurrence: Minnesota — prairies, clearings, and rocky places. Grows on rocky cliffs along Lake Superior; general — temperate central North America.

Composite Family

225. Flat-top White Aster (*A. umbellatus*). Stout aster of wet places. It is often 4 to 6 feet tall. Flower heads are white or cream-colored and are arranged in large, flat clusters. The numerous leaves taper toward both ends. Occurrence: Minnesota — throughout in marshes,

180

brushy swamps, and roadside ditches; general — mostly eastern temperate North America.

Composite Family

226. Heath Aster (*A. ericoides*). Also called Frost-weed Aster. Common, white aster of dry prairies and other open places. The bushy, grayish plants, usually 1 to 2 feet tall, have many small, white flower heads. They are about ½ inch across and are arranged in dense, often 1-sided clusters. Heath Aster frequently grows in patches. Occurrence: Minnesota — mostly in the south and west; general — eastern and central temperate North America.

Composite Family

227. Side-flowering Aster (*A. lateriflorus*). Also called Calico Aster. A robust, clumped, and much branched aster of swamp edges and brushy places. It is often as tall as 3 feet. The small, white-rayed flower heads are about ½ inch across and are usually borne on one side of the upper branches. Centers of heads range from yellow to purplish, giving a "calico" effect. Occurrence: Minnesota — mostly in brushy places in the hardwood forest areas; general — temperate eastern North America.

226. Heath Aster. Autumn.

227. Side-flowering Aster. Autumn.

181

228. Boltonia. Late summer; autumn.

229. Daisy Fleabane. Spring; summer.

Composite Family

BOLTONIA (*Boltonia*)

228. Boltonia (*B. asteroides*). Robust, asterlike perennial of damp prairies, swales, and edges of streams. The branched stems are often in clumps 3 to 5 feet tall. The flower heads, about 1 inch across, are numerous, have yellow, hemispherical centers and narrow, usually white rays. Occasionally the rays are pale pink, purple, or blue. The seedlike fruits (achenes) differ from those of the asters and fleabanes by having no tuft of hairs at one end. Occurrence: Minnesota — mostly in south and east; general — eastern U.S.

Boltonia is sometimes grown in gardens.

Composite Family

FLEABANE (*Erigeron*)

229. Daisy Fleabane (*E. philadelphicus*). Hairy plant, usually biennial, of moist meadows and roadsides. The flower heads, which are about 1 inch across, have many threadlike white, pink, or purplish rays surrounding a yellow center. Stem is erect, usually 1 to 2 feet tall, and has a tuft of slender roots at the base. The rather wide leaves clasp the stem. Occurrence: Minnesota — throughout; general —widely distributed in temperate North America.

The **Rough Fleabane** (*E. strigosus*) has similar but smaller flower heads, about ½ inch across, with white rays. Stem leaves are narrow and not markedly clasping at the base. This widely distributed plant prefers dry fields and roadsides. It is usually an annual.

230. Plantain-leaved Everlasting. Summer.

Composite Family

EVERLASTING (*Antennaria*)

230. Plantain-leaved Everlasting (*A. plantaginifolia*). Grayish perennial with a rosette of spoon-shaped leaves, usually 2 to 4 inches long with 3 or 5 nerves running the length of the blade. The flower heads, which have no rays and are covered with silky hairs, are clustered at the end of a slender stem. They are usually unisexual. Plants spread by runners, often forming patches. Occurrence: Minnesota — dry, open places, especially in the west and south; general — eastern U.S.

Several other kinds, sometimes called Ladies' Tobacco, have smaller leaves with a single midrib and are considered to be varieties of *A. neglecta*. They include the **Canada Everlasting**, with leaves green and hairless above, and the **Field Everlasting**, with leaves covered on both sides by soft, gray hairs. Both form patches in pastures and other dry, open places.

231. Pearly Everlasting. Summer.

232. Sweet Everlasting. Summer.

PEARLY EVERLASTING
(*Anaphalis*)

231. Pearly Everlasting (*A. margaritacea*). Erect, often clumped perennial, usually 1 to 2 feet tall, of undisturbed open or brushy uplands. Stems and elongate leaves are woolly with white hairs. The small flower. heads are clustered at the top of the stem. The tiny, yellow flowers are enclosed by many white, papery bracts which might be mistaken for petals. Occurrence: Minnesota — most common in the north and east, often where there have been forest fires; general — temperate North America and Asia.

Pearly Everlasting is sometimes picked and dried. for winter bouquets.

Composite Family

SWEET EVERLASTING
(*Gnaphalium*)

232. Sweet Everlasting (*G. obtusifolium*). Erect annual, generally similar to the preceding species but with more elongate flower heads having brownish, papery bracts. The herbage is fragrant. Occurrence: Minnesota — mostly in the north in sandy places; general — temperate eastern North America.

The Menomini Indians burned the leaves of the plant to make sweet-scented smoke which they used to revive people from fainting spells and to discourage ghosts that caused bad dreams.

184

Composite Family

BONESET (*Eupatorium*)

233. Joe-Pye Weed (*E. maculatum*). Robust perennial, usually 3 to 5 feet tall, of swamps and ditch banks. The purplish flower heads are in a flattish cluster. The toothed leaves generally are in whorls of 4 or 5 and the stem is often spotted with purple. Occurrence: Minnesota — throughout in moist places; general — temperate North America.

Tincture of the roots was used medicinally by early American physicians and the plant was gathered by Chippewa Indians to make "strengthening baths."

Composite Family

234. Sweet Joe-Pye Weed (*E. purpureum*). Similar to Joe-Pye Weed but with flower heads in a somewhat rounded or domed cluster. Leaves are mostly in whorls of 3 or 4. Occurrence: Minnesota — most common in the east and north-central portion, often in thickets and along edges of woods; general — eastern temperate North America.

Joe Pye is thought to have been an Indian physician who made use of this plant in New England.

233. Joe-Pye Weed. Summer; autumn.

234. Sweet Joe-Pye Weed. Summer; autumn.

185

235. Boneset. Summer; autumn.

236. White Snakeroot. Summer; autumn.

Composite Family

235. Boneset (*E. perfoliatum*). Coarse, hairy perennial, usually 2 to 3 feet tall, with a conspicuous, flattish cluster of small, white flower heads and opposite, elongate leaves that are joined at the base. Occurrence: Minnesota — throughout in swamps and damp pastures; general — eastern temperate North America.

Boneset tea was a popular folk medicine used for diseases as diverse as common colds, malaria, and break-bone fever (dengue). This last use may account for the common name.

Composite Family

236. White Snakeroot (*E. rugosum*). Perennial of shady places. The branched stems, usually 2 to 3 feet tall, bear opposite leaves with toothed, oval blades and flattish clusters of pure white flower heads. Occurrence: Minnesota — mostly in hardwood forests of the south; general — eastern temperate North America.

The herbage contains trematol, which is poisonous to livestock and which is excreted in cow's milk. Such milk, if consumed by humans, causes "milk sickness." This is the disease from which Lincoln's mother, Nancy Hanks, died. In pioneer times cattle were often pastured in newly cleared woodlands where Snakeroot thrives.

Composite Family

BLAZING STAR (*Liatris*)

237. Dotted Blazing Star (*L. punc-*

186

237. Dotted Blazing Star. Summer; autumn.

tata). Low-growing perennial of prairies. The clumped, erect stems are often less than 1 foot tall and end in a spikelike cluster of purple flower heads. Each head usually has fewer than 8 flowers and the erect bracts enclosing them are sharply pointed. The narrow leaves are pitted or dotted beneath. Occurrence: Minnesota — mostly in the south and west on dry prairies; general — upper Midwest and Great Plains.

The stems of this and the following species usually rise from a thick corm.

Composite Family

238. Tall Blazing Star (*L. pycnostachya*). Perennial of moist prairies. The unbranched stems are often 3 to 4 feet tall and end in a long spike of small, purple flower heads, each with fewer than 8 flowers. The bracts at the base of the flower heads (involucre bracts) are pointed and the tips curve outward. Occurrence: Minnesota — prairies, mostly

in the south and west; general — central U.S.

This species, including a white variety, is sometimes grown in gardens under the name Kansas Gay Feather.

238. Tall Blazing Star. Summer; autumn.

239. Rough Blazing Star. Summer; autumn.

240. Western Ironweed. Summer; autumn.

Composite Family

239. Rough Blazing Star (*L. aspera*). Perennial, usually 1 to 3 feet tall, with unbranched stems ending in a spikelike cluster of purple flower heads. Each head contains more than 15 flowers. The bracts surrounding the flowers are rounded and have a thin, papery margin. Occurrence: Minnesota — prairies and open woods, mostly in the south and west; general — temperate eastern North America.

Composite Family

IRONWEED (*Vernonia*)

240. Western Ironweed (*V. fasciculata*). Clumped perennial of marshes and wet prairies. It has deep purple flower heads in a spreading cluster. Stems, usually 2 to 4 feet tall, are often reddish and the elongate leaves are hairless and sharply toothed. Occurrence: Minnesota — mostly in the south and west; general — central U.S. and adjacent Canada.

Ironweed often thrives in wet pastures where cattle graze around it.

Composite Family

NODDING THISTLE (*Carduus*)

241. Nodding Thistle (*C. nutans*). A recent, prickly addition to Minnesota's bouquet of wild flowers. This beautiful Eurasian Thistle, which grows up to 4 feet tall, has long-stalked, purple flower heads 2 to 3 inches across. The flowers are enclosed in spine-tipped bracts, the outermost of which are bent backward. Occurrence: Minnesota — occasional in old fields and prairies in the south, where it is becoming in-

188

creasingly abundant; general—widely but sparingly distributed in North America.

Composite Family

THISTLE (*Cirsium*)

242. Bull Thistle (*C. vulgare*). A robust, hairy biennial growing to 4 feet or more and having elongate, lobed leaves with crinkled margins and armed with spines. Wings extend down the stem from the base of the leaves. Flower heads are pale purple and often 2 inches or more across. The bracts of the flower head are tipped with stout, yellowish spines. Occurrence: widely distributed in Minnesota and elsewhere in North America in pastures, waste places, and along roads. A native of Eurasia.

241. Nodding Thistle. Summer.

242. Bull Thistle. Summer.

189

243. Field Thistle. Summer.

244. Swamp Thistle. Summer; autumn.

Composite Family

243. Field Thistle (*C. discolor*). Robust thistle, commonly 3 to 6 feet tall, with elongate, lobed leaves that are nearly flat. The undersurface of the leaves is covered with white hairs and the margins have weak spines. Flower heads are pale purple, up to 2 inches wide, and have involucre bracts tipped by long, slender spines that stand out at an angle to the heads. Occurrence: Minnesota — dry fields, roadsides, and waste places; general — eastern U.S. and adjacent Canada.

Composite Family

244. Swamp Thistle (*C. muticum*). Stout thistle, usually 3 to 6 feet tall, of open and brushy swamps. The elongate, lobed leaves are almost flat, green, and nearly hairless when fully grown. Spines on the leaf margins are weak. The wine-purple flower heads are about 1½ inches across and have involucre bracts without spines at the tips. Occurrence: Minnesota — throughout in swamps except in the south and southwest; general — temperate eastern North America.

Composite Family

245. Flodman's Thistle (*C. flodmani*). Low perennial thistle, usually 1 to 2 feet tall, of prairies, plains, and dry, open places. The elongate stem leaves are cut into spine-tipped lobes, but basal leaves may be without lobes. Leaves are woolly with matted, white hairs, at least on the undersurface. The beautiful wine-red flower heads are about 2 inches across. Occurrence: Minnesota — prairies, mostly in the

246. Common Dandelion. Spring; summer.

south and west; general — Great Plains.

245. Flodman's Thistle. Summer.

Composite Family

DANDELION (*Taraxacum*)

246. Common Dandelion (*T. officinale*). One of man's persistent companions. It thrives despite being stepped on, mowed, or grazed, and soon returns after being decimated with herbicides. Leaves of the flat rosette have backward-pointing teeth — in French "dent de lion" — hence the name. They rise from a taproot. The yellow flower heads open in the morning and close in the evening. They attract bees and other insects but can set fruits without pollination. The tawny or pale brown fruits (achenes) are windborne on silken parasols. Occurrence: this European species is widely distributed in North America.

The **Red-seeded Dandelion** (*T. erythrospermum*) is similar but usually somewhat smaller. It has deeply cut leaves and reddish-brown "seeds." It is also Eurasian and widespread.

191

247. Common Sow Thistle. Summer.

248. Blue Lettuce. Summer.

Composite Family

SOW THISTLE (*Sonchus*)

247. Common Sow Thistle (*S. arvensis*). An erect perennial with stems usually 2 to 4 feet tall and yellow flower heads resembling but usually somewhat larger than those of dandelions. The elongate leaves are lobed and have weak prickles. The juice is milky and the plant spreads by rootstalks, often forming patches. Occurrence: A European plant widely distributed in North America, especially along roads. Before modern herbicides were used, it was a persistent weed of grain fields and difficult to control. In the Red River Valley fields were once yellow with its blossoms.

Composite Family

LETTUCE (*Lactuca*)

248. Blue Lettuce (*L. pulchella*). Pe-

192

rennial, usually 1 to 2 feet tall, of roadsides, prairies, and brushy places. The bright blue flower heads, about ¾ inch across, are shaped like those of the dandelion. The elongate, often bluish-green leaves are lobed and have milky juice. Occurrence: Minnesota — throughout but uncommon in the northeast; general — central and western North America.

Composite Family

249. Prickly Lettuce (*L. serriola*). Weedy annual or biennial that is probably the ancestor of cultivated lettuce. The erect and branched stem, usually 2 to 3 feet tall, bears numerous small, pale yellow flower heads and elongate leaves with weak prickles. The gray, seedlike fruits become wind-borne by a tuft of silky hairs. Occurrence: a European species that is widely distributed in North America.

In spring, when only basal leaves

249. Prickly Lettuce. Summer.

are present, these may turn on edge and become oriented in a north-south direction to form a "compass plant."

249a. Prickly Lettuce as a Compass Plant. Spring.

250. Canada Lettuce. Summer.

Composite Family

GOAT'S BEARD (*Tragopogon*)

251. Goat's Beard (*T. dubius*). Common plant of roadsides. The erect stems, 1 to 3 feet tall, end in pale yellow flower heads much like those of a large dandelion. They have long, green bracts standing behind the shorter, yellow rays. The flower heads face the sun. Leaves are elongate, parallel-veined and without teeth or lobes. The rounded heads of parachute-winged fruits are sometimes gathered for winter bouquets after being sprayed with thin lacquer to fix the fruits in place. Occurrence: this European biennial is widely naturalized in North America.

Goat's Beard is one of the few Dicots that have parallel-veined leaves. The juice is milky.

Composite Family

250. Canada Lettuce (*L. canadensis*). Native annual or biennial, sometimes growing to 6 feet. It has numerous small, deep-yellow flower heads and nearly black, seedlike achenes. Leaves are elongate and lobed or toothed but not prickly. Occurrence: Minnesota — throughout in well-drained, open and brushy places; general — temperate eastern North America.

Composite Family

CHICORY (*Cichorium*)

252. Chicory (*C. intybus*). Also called Blue Sailors. Perennial, usually 1 to 3 feet tall, of roadsides and old fields. The bright blue flower heads are 1 to 1½ inches across and set close against the upright stems. (Flower color varies with age and locality, and may be almost white, pale blue, or pinkish.) The thick taproot, when roasted, has long been used as a coffee substitute or additive. Occurrence: a Eurasian plant widely distributed in North America.

The name is very old and of Egyptian or Arabic origin.

252. Chicory. Summer.

251a. Goat's Beard in fruit. Summer.

1. Goat's Beard. Spring; summer.

253. Pale Agoseris. Summer.

254. Rattlesnake-root. Summer.

AGOSERIS (*Agoseris*)

253. Pale Agoseris (*A. glauca*). Also called Prairie Dandelion. Perennial of moist prairies. It has yellow, dandelionlike flower heads at the end of slender leafless stalks. The leaves are basal, elongate, and mostly without teeth or lobes. They have parallel veins. The plant is often pale bluish-green and has milky juice. Occurrence: Minnesota — prairies, mostly in the west; general — prairies of western North America.

Composite Family

RATTLESNAKE-ROOT
(*Prenanthes*)

254. Rattlesnake-root (*P. alba*). Perennial of open woods and shady roadsides. It is usually 2 to 3 feet tall and has elongate clusters of nodding flower heads that are white, yellowish, or purple-tinged. Stems and leaves are bluish-green. The leaves are stalked and the leaf blades variously lobed and often widest toward the base. Bracts of the flower heads are hairless. Occurrence: Minnesota — throughout, except in the southwest; general — temperate eastern North America.

Composite Family

255. Glaucous Rattlesnake-root (*P. racemosa*). Perennial of prairies. The erect stem, usually 1 to 3 feet tall, ends in a spikelike cluster of purplish flower heads. Each flower head is on a short stalk and directed upward. Bracts of the flower heads are hairy. Leaves are oval to oblong and not lobed. Juice is milky. Occurrence: Minnesota — mostly in

196

the south and west; general — temperate eastern North America.

Composite Family

HAWKWEED (*Hieracium*)

256. Canada Hawkweed (*H. canadense*). Perennial, 1 to 3 feet tall, of open woods and fields. The leafy stem ends in an open cluster of deep 'yellow, dandelionlike flower heads, each about 1 inch across. Leaves are elongate and usually have a few coarse teeth. Occurrence: Minnesota — mostly in the north and east in sandy areas; general — temperate North America.

256. Canada Hawkweed. Summer.

Composite Family

257. Orange Hawkweed (*H. aurantiacum*). Also called King-devil and Devil's Paint Brush. Low perennial, usually less than 1 foot tall. The hairy, leafless stem is topped by a spreading cluster of bright red-orange flower heads, each about ¾ inch across. Leaves are elliptical and in a basal cluster. The plants spread by rootstalks and runners and often grow in patches. Occurrence: Minnesota — most common in the northeast where it forms red-orange patches along roads and in clearings; general — naturalized here and there throughout temperate North America. Often considered a weed. In Eurasia it is an alpine plant.

257. Orange Hawkweed. Summer.

255. Glaucous Rattlesnake-root. Summer.

Composite Family
HAWK'S-BEARD (*Crepis*)

258. Hawk's-beard (*C. tectorum*). A slender-stemmed annual, usually 1 to 2 feet tall, with narrow, elongate leaves or leaf segments. It has spreading clusters of pale yellow flower heads, each about ½ inch across. The seedlike achenes are tipped with a tuft of white hairs. Occurrence: Minnesota — open, disturbed soils throughout; general — this and several quite similar European species are widely distributed in North America, mostly as weedy plants. *C. tectorum* has become common in Minnesota in recent years.

Cattail Family
CATTAIL (*Typha*)

259. Narrow-leaved Cattail (*T. glauca* [in the sense of Gray's *Manual*, 1950]). Clumped perennial, often 6 feet or more tall, of marshes, shores, and shallow water. Leaves are elongate, about ½ inch wide, and the minute flowers are in a dense spike. In this species the lower (pistillate) portion of the spike is separated from the upper (staminate) portion by a stretch of smooth stem. The staminate flowers fall soon after shedding pollen, leaving only rough stem. Seeds are wind-borne on a tuft of down. Occurrence: Minnesota — throughout, but not common in the northeast; general — northern and eastern U.S. and adjacent Canada. This species has become increasingly abundant in Minnesota since the 1930s.

The **Common Cattail** (*T. latifolia*) is shorter, has wider leaves, and has no gap between the staminate

258. Hawk's-beard. Summer.

259. Narrow-leaved Cattail. Summer.

260. Broad-leaved Arrowhead. Summer.

and pistillate parts of the spike. Widely distributed and common.

Water-plantain Family

ARROWHEAD (*Sagittaria*)

260. Broad-leaved Arrowhead (*S. latifolia*). Also called Wapato and Duck Potato. Perennial, usually 1 to 2 feet tall, of open marshes, shores, and shallow water. The flowers have 3 white petals. Leaves are mostly basal with arrowhead-shaped blades.

In late summer starchy tubers, an inch or more in diameter, are produced in the bottom mud. Indians called them Swan Potatoes and dried them for winter food. Occurrence: Minnesota—throughout; general—much of North America.

There are several other species, some of which have elongate or elliptical leaf blades. The tubers are dug and eaten by muskrats but are usually too deep in the mud for ducks.

261 Wild Rice. Summer; early autumn.

Grass Family

WILD RICE (*Zizania*)

261. Wild Rice (*Z. aquatica*). This aquatic grass was once a staple food of Minnesota Indians. It grows in shallow waters of lakes and streams, and usually stands 3 to 6 feet tall when mature. Growth begins as submerged and then floating, ribbonlike leaves. In summer the stem emerges from the water and flow-

ers. By early autumn the grains ripen. They can be harvested by knocking them into a canoe with short hand flails. Occurrence: Minnesota— common in the north, where there are 30,000 acres in wild, self-seeding stands; general—Great Lakes region and southern Manitoba. Occasional elsewhere. Widely planted as a water-fowl food plant.

The parched and processed seed

is widely used as a gourmet food. In recent years improved strains of Wild Rice have been developed and grown in paddies to augment the harvest from wild stands.

Arum Family

JACK-IN-THE-PULPIT (*Arisaema*)

262. Jack-in-the-Pulpit (*A. triphyllum*). Also called Indian Turnip. Erect, often reddish perennial of moist woods. Usually about 1 foot tall. Leaves are compound with 3 pointed leaflets. The small flowers are crowded near the base of a club-like spadix (Jack) that is enclosed in a narrow, funnel-shaped structure (spathe) that has an overhanging flap at the top, the old-style "pulpit." In late summer a cluster of bright red berries is exposed by the withering of the spathe. Occurrence: Minnesota — throughout; general — temperate eastern North America.

The thickened root (corm) at the base of the plant, and to a lesser extent other plant parts, contain needlelike calcium oxalate crystals, which cause a burning sensation if eaten.

262. Jack-in-the-Pulpit. Spring; summer.

262a. Jack-in-the-Pulpit in fruit. Summer.

Arum Family

WILD CALLA (*Calla*)

263. Wild Calla (*C. palustris*). Perennial of swamps and quiet, shallow waters. Shiny, heart-shaped leaves are clustered at the end of the long, yellow rootstalk. The small flowers are crowded in a clublike spadix behind which is the white, elliptical spathe. In late summer the spadix becomes a cluster of red berries. Occurrence: Minnesota—mostly in forested areas of the north; general—circumpolar and in North America from subarctic south to temperate regions.

The plant, like most members of the Arum Family, contains acrid, needlelike crystals of calcium oxalate.

263. Wild Calla. Spring; summer.

264. Skunk Cabbage. Spring; summer.

Arum Family

SKUNK CABBAGE (*Symplocarpus*)

264. Skunk Cabbage (*S. foetidus*). Among the first wild flowers of spring and the oddest. The pointed, brown or purplish spathe, 4 to 6 inches high, encloses a clublike stem, the spadix, on which are tiny flowers. Pollinating insects enter this botanical tepee, probably attracted by odor, warmth, and shelter. Later the fruit, much like a small-stalked and roughened potato, develops beneath the clump of very large summer leaves. The fruit contains large, acrid seeds in a bland pulp. The entire plant has a skunky odor. Occurrence: Minnesota—along the eastern border in swamps and seepage areas; general—temperate eastern North America. Also in Asia.

Arum Family

SWEET FLAG (*Acorus*)

265. Sweet Flag (*A. calamus*). Clumped perennial of swamps and shallow water. Usually 2 to 4 feet tall. Its erect, swordlike leaves are much like those of Blue Flag, except they are yellowish-green, rather than bluish-green, and aromatic. The small flowers, and later the dried fruits, are in a dense cluster (spadix) near the top of the flattened, leaflike stem. The spathe, conspicuous in many members of the Arum Family, in Sweet Flag is the tapering upper part of the stem. Occurrence: Minnesota — throughout, often in and along streams; general—temperate North America. Also in Eurasia.

265. Sweet Flag. Summer.

Sweet Flag has had considerable use in Indian and folk medicine. In pioneer times the rootstalks were thinly sliced and candied.

DAY FLOWER (*Commelina*)

266. Asiatic Day Flower (*C. communis*). Low, spreading annual with declining, spreading stems that root at the nodes. Upright stems are usually less than 1 foot tall. Leaves are oblong or oval and pointed. The flowers are about ½ inch across, with 2 blue petals and 1 smaller, white petal. They last only a day. Occurrence: a native of Asia, widely naturalized in eastern U.S. in shady places and dooryards.

The generic name, *Commelina*, which was assigned by Linnaeus, refers to the Commelin brothers, early Dutch botanists, two of whom (the blue petals) were productive botanists and the third (the white petal) who did little.

266. Asiatic Day Flower. Summer.

267. Western Spiderwort. Spring; summer.

Spiderwort Family

SPIDERWORT (*Tradescantia*)

267. Western Spiderwort (*T. occidentalis*). Perennial, usually 1 to 2 feet tall, with erect, leafy stems, grasslike leaves, and clustered 3-petaled flowers. Flowers are usually blue but sometimes pink, white, or pale purple. They are about 1¼ inches across and on hot summer days wilt by noon. The green sepals are sticky with glandular hairs. Herbage is somewhat fleshy and has sticky juice that can be seen as filaments, much like those of a spider web, if segments of a leaf are slowly pulled apart. Occurrence: Minnesota—open, grassy places mostly in the center and northwest; general—prairies and plains of western North America.

The **Bracted Spiderwort** (*T. bracteata*) is similar, but the sepals are covered with a mixture of soft, normal hairs and hairs tipped by sticky glands.

Lily Family

WHITE CAMAS (*Zygadenus*)

268. White Camas (*Z. elegans*). Perennial of moist prairies and meadows. The stem, usually 1 to 2 feet tall, rises from a bulb. On it grasslike leaves are crowded near the base. Flowers are white, tinged on the back with green, purple, or brown. They are ½ to ¾ inch across and have 6 perianth parts, each with a spotlike gland near the base. Occurrence: Minnesota — prairies, mostly in the south and west; general—western North America.

White Camas is poisonous to grazing animals.

268. White Camas. Late spring; summer.

269. Tawny Day Lily. Summer.

Lily Family

DAY LILY (*Hemerocallis*)

269. Tawny Day Lily (*H. fulva*). Perennial of roads and open places, especially near old home sites. The large, tawny-orange flowers, about 4 inches long, are at the end of a

270. Meadow Garlic. Spring; summer.

leafless stalk. They last but a single day and do not produce seeds. The clumped basal leaves are keeled and somewhat arching. There is a clump of thick roots, and the plants spread by short rootstalks to form patches. Occurrence: this native of eastern Asia was imported as a garden plant. It is widely naturalized in North America. The double form, var. *kwanso*, has also escaped from gardens.

In China the flower buds are used in cooking. It is likely that Day Lily has been spread along highways by road maintenance equipment.

Lily Family

ONION (*Allium*)

270. Meadow Garlic (*A. canadense*). Low perennial, usually less than a foot tall, of prairies and meadows. The elongate, solid leaves and flowering stems rise from a bulb. Flowers are 6-parted, usually pale purple, and in an umbel. Often brown bulblets replace some or all of the flowers. Occurrence: Minnesota—mostly in the south; general—eastern U.S.

206

271. Prairie Onion. Spring; summer.

This and other native onions were used by Indians for flavoring. Its Algonquian name, Shig-gau-ga-whin-zheeg, means "skunk weed." From it comes Chicago, meaning "place where wild onions grow."

Lily Family

271. Prairie Onion (*A. stellatum*). Has slender, solid leaves and stems, and erect umbels of small pink or rosy flowers. The bulb has papery scales. Occurrence: Minnesota—prairies and meadows throughout but most common in the south and west; general—central North America.

Wild Leek (*A. tricoccum*), an onion of hardwood forests, has long, flat leaves that are shiny and pointed. They have a strong garlic odor. In summer, after the leaves are gone, an umbel of whitish flowers is produced.

Lily Family

LILY (*Lilium*)

272. Turk's-cap Lily (*L. superbum*). A beautiful wild flower. The erect stem, usually 3 to 5 feet tall, rises from a scaly bulb. It has several whorls of leaves and 1 or more conspicuous, nodding flowers, each with 6 backward-curving perianth parts, 3 petals, and 3 sepals. They are yellow to orange-red, dotted with purple, and about 3 inches across. Occurrence: Minnesota — damp meadows, roadsides and brushy places; widespread but mostly in the east; general — temperate eastern North America.

The Turk's-cap Lily is now uncommon, largely because of farming of meadows and careful maintenance of roadsides.

272. Turk's-cap Lily. Summer.

273. Wood Lily. Summer.

Lily Family

273. Wood Lily (*L. philadelphicum*). The orange-red flowers are erect and top the stem, which is usually 1 to 2 feet tall. Leaves are scattered along the stem, except the uppermost, which are whorled. Flowers are 2 to 3 inches across and spotted inside with purple. Occurrence: Minnesota — throughout in open and brushy places but most common in the pine-forest country of the north; general — temperate North America.

Lily Family

TROUT LILY (*Erythronium*)

274. White Trout Lily (*E. albidum*). Also called Dog-tooth Violet. Low woodland perennial with elliptical, pointed leaves that are basal and often marked with brown or purple. They are somewhat fleshy. The

208

flower, at the end of a leafless stem, is nodding, 1 to 2 inches across, and has 6 pointed perianth parts that are backward-curved. They are white, sometimes tinged with pink or blue. Occurrence: Minnesota — most common in hardwood forests of the southeast, often growing in patches; general — temperate eastern North America.

The **Yellow Trout Lily** (*E. americanum*) is similar but has yellow flowers. It is uncommon in eastern Minnesota.

Lily Family

275. Minnesota Trout Lily (*E. propullans*). Low perennial of moist woods, especially river bottoms and ravines. Leaves are similar but smaller than those of the White Trout Lily. The flower is pale pink and about ½ inch across. Occurrence: Minnesota — known only from a few locations in the southeast; general — also reported in recent years from Ontario.

This rare wild flower was described in 1871 from a specimen collected by Mary B. Hedges, teacher of botany at Faribault. She sent it to botanist Asa Gray at Harvard, who gave it its botanical name. Some plants have been transplanted to the University of Minnesota Arboretum at Chanhassen where they can be seen in bloom in spring.

274. White Trout Lily. Spring.

275. Minnesota Trout Lily. Spring.

209

276. Clintonia. Spring; summer.

Lily Family

CLINTONIA (*Clintonia*)

276. Clintonia (*C. borealis*). Also called Blue-bead Lily. Perennial of damp woods and swampy, brushy places. It is usually less than 1 foot tall and has a basal clump of 3 to 5 shiny, elliptical leaves. A spreading cluster of pale yellow, 6-parted flowers is borne at the top of a slender, leafless stem. Leaf margins have silky, white hairs. The flowers are followed by spherical blue berries, about ⅓ inch across. Occurrence: Minnesota—mostly in the coniferous forest region. of the north; general—temperate eastern North America.

Menomini Indians placed the leaves on dog bites to "draw out the poison" and Chippewa squaws made artistic patterns by biting the leaf blades.

Lily Family

FALSE SOLOMON'S SEAL
(*Smilacina*)

277. Star-flowered False Solomon's Seal (*S. stellata*). The elongate and often arching stem bears wide leaves that taper to both ends. It terminates in a cluster of small, 6-parted, white flowers, each of which is connected to the stem by an unbranched stalk. The flowers are followed by berries, at first striped green and brown but red when ripe. Occurrence: Minnesota—open woods, prairies, and along roads and railways throughout; general—widespread in subarctic and temperate North America.

The **Three-leaved False Solomon's Seal** (*S. trifolia*) has flowers and fruits similar to the preceding. However, it is a short, erect plant, about 6 inches tall, of wet woods and bogs. It is shown in the photograph of *Arethusa*.

277. Star-flowered False Solomon's Seal. Spring; summer.

Lily Family

278. False Spikenard (*S. racemosa*). Woodland perennial with unbranched stems, often arching, usually 1 to 2 feet long. The stem bears alternate elliptical leaves and ends in a dense cluster of many small, white flowers. On each inflorescence branch there are several flowers and later red berries. The stem rises from an elongate rootstalk. Leaves are hairy beneath. Occurrence: Minnesota—widely distributed and common in moist, rich forests; general—temperate North America, except in the far west.

The scars on the rootstalk, marking the attachment position of former aerial stems, are similar to those of True Solomon's Seal (*Polygonatum*).

278. False Spikenard. Late spring; summer.

Lily Family

FALSE LILY-OF-THE-VALLEY
(*Maianthemum*)

279. False Lily-of-the-Valley (*M. canadense*). Low plant, usually 3 to 6 inches tall, of woods and woodland edges. The white flowers are in small, upright clusters. Each flower has 2 petals and 2 sepals, differing from most other monocots, which have flower parts in 3's. The leaves are pointed, oval to oblong, and heart-shaped or abruptly narrowed at the base. There are usually 2 leaves on the stem, but individual leaves are also produced along the slender rootstalk. The fruit is a small, pale red berry. Occurrence: Minnesota—throughout in wooded areas; general—temperate eastern North America.

279. False Lily-of-the-Valley. Spring.

280. Large-flowered Bellwort. Spring.

Lily Family

BELLWORT (*Uvularia*)

280. Large-flowered Bellwort (*U. grandiflora*). Spring wild flower of moist woods. Blossoming clumps are usually less than 1 foot tall, but later the forking stem lengthens. The pale yellow, 6-parted flower is nodding and 1 to 2 inches long. Perianth parts are often twisted. Leaves have the stem passing through them near the base. The fruit is a capsule containing seed. Occurrence: Minnesota—throughout in wooded areas but not in the southwest; general—temperate eastern North America.

Lily Family

281. Sessile-leaved Bellwort (*U. sessilifolia*). Also called Wild Oats. Woodland perennial, with leafy

212

stems less than 10 inches long. It often spreads by rootstalks to form patches. The elongate leaves taper to both ends and have no stalks. Flowers are nodding, 6-parted, and ½ to 1 inch long. They are pale yellow or cream-colored. The fruit is a 3-sided pod. Occurrence: Minnesota — throughout except in the southwestern and extreme western prairie region; general — temperate eastern North America.

Lily Family

SOLOMON'S SEAL (*Polygonatum*)

282. Smooth Solomon's Seal (*P. biflorum*). Perennial with elongate, usually arching stems, often 2 to 3 feet long. Leaves are elliptical, not hairy on the veins beneath, and arranged in 2 ranks. The small, white flowers are ½ to ¾ inch long. They, and later the dark blue or black berries, hang in clusters from the leaf axils. Occurrence: Minnesota — throughout in wooded areas; general — temperate eastern North America.

Hairy Solomon's Seal (*P. pubescens*) is similar but has smaller

281. Sessile-leaved Bellwort. Spring.

yellowish-green flowers and leaves with hairy veins beneath.

Solomon's Seal has an ancient name. Seal refers to the circular scars on the rootstalk where stems of former years were attached.

282. Smooth Solomon's Seal. Late spring; summer.

283. Large-flowered Trillium. Spring..

Lily Family

TRILLIUM (*Trillium*)

283. Large-flowered Trillium (*T. grandiflorum*). Also called Wake Robin. Common and conspicuous spring wild flower of woods and woodland edges. The erect stems, usually about 1 foot tall, end in a whorl of 3 wide, pointed leaves and a single, erect flower that has 3 white petals, 2 to 3 inches long. The flower may be pink or purple with age. The fruit is a black berry. Occurrence: Minnesota—moist, fertile woods in east, center, and north; general—temperate eastern North America.

The **Snow Trillium** (*T. nivale*) has similar upright flowers but is smaller, usually less than 6 inches tall, with petals 1 to 2 inches long. It blossoms early and is found in the southeast.

284. Declining Trillium. Spring.

214

285. Yellow Star Grass. Spring; summer.

Lily Family

284. Declining Trillium (*T. flexipes*). The plant is much like that of the Large-flowered Trillium, but the flower is at the end of a downward-sloping stalk, 2 to 4 inches long, and is hidden beneath the leaves. The white petals are shorter than 2 inches. Occurrence: Minnesota—mostly in the southern third; general—upper eastern U.S.

The **Nodding Trillium** (*T. cernuum*) is similar but has a nodding flower on a short stalk, less than 1½ inches long. It is found throughout Minnesota except in some of the southwestern prairie counties.

Amaryllis Family

YELLOW STAR GRASS (*Hypoxis*)

285. Yellow Star Grass (*H. hirsuta*). In late spring some meadows are starred with its bright yellow flowers. This plant, usually shorter than 8 inches, has grassy leaves on which are soft hairs. The leaves and slender stem rise from a small corm. Flowers are in a few-flowered umbel. Each has 6 perianth parts and is ½ to ¾ inch wide. Occurrence: Minnesota—throughout in damp meadows and prairies, except in the northeast; general—temperate eastern North America.

215

286. Blue Flag. Spring; early summer.

Iris Family

IRIS or FLAG (*Iris*)

286. Blue Flag (*I. versicolor*). Perennial of marshes and shallow water. Leaves are upright, swordlike, and 2-ranked. The branched stem, up to 2 feet tall, bears conspicuous, blue flowers that are about 3 inches across. They have 3 spreading, downward-bent sepals and 3 shorter, ascending petals. The fruit is a pod 1½ to 2½ inches long. Occurrence: Minnesota – widespread, the common iris in the north; general – upper eastern U.S. and adjacent Canada.

Shreve's Blue Flag (*I. virginica* var. *shrevei*) is similar but characterized by larger pods. It is found mostly in southern Minnesota.

Rootstalks of blue flags contain emetic and cathartic substances, and are poisonous to cattle.

216

Iris Family.

287. Yellow Flag (*I. pseudacorus*). Robust perennial of wet places; often 3 to 4 feet tall. The clumped basal leaves are erect and swordlike and the large, pale yellow flowers are on a branched, flowering stem. Occurrence: a native of Europe that came to America as a garden plant but has become widely naturalized in eastern temperate North America. In Minnesota it is found occasionally in marshes and along lakeshores and streams.

Yellow Flag grows along the River Lys in Flanders and because of this, Marie-Victorin, French-Canadian botanist, considered it to be the original model for the fleur-de-lis of French heraldry.

Iris Family

BLUE-EYED GRASS
(*Sisyrhinchium*)

288. Blue-eyed Grass (*S. montanum*). Perennial with grasslike leaves. Commonly tufted and less than 1 foot tall. The violet-purple flowers have 6 similar, spreading perianth parts. They are usually about ¾ inch across and in a small cluster near the top of the flat, narrow stem. Roots are fibrous. Occurrence: Minnesota—widespread in open places, often on sandy soil; general—much of temperate North America.

The **Prairie Blue-eyed Grass** (*S. campestre*) is similar but has pale blue or white flowers. It is a midwestern species that is widespread in Minnesota.

287. Yellow Flag. Spring; early summer.

288. Blue-eyed Grass. Spring.

289. Stemless Lady-slipper. Spring; early summer.

Orchid Family

LADY-SLIPPER (*Cypripedium*)

289. Stemless Lady-slipper (*C. acaule*). Also called Moccasin Flower. Perennial with 2 oval, basal leaves and a flower stalk usually 6 to 8 inches tall. It is topped by the showy rose-purple flower. The lip or "slipper" is about 2 inches long and cleft or split above. As in other lady-slippers, the flower is marvelously modified as an insect trap. Insects that enter the lip can escape only by going upward past the modified stamens and pistil, thereby pollinating the flowers. Occurrence: Minnesota—mostly in the north on acid soils (pH 4 to 5) of bogs, marshes, and coniferous forests; general—eastern U.S. and adjacent Canada.

290. Showy Lady-slipper. Late spring; summer.

Orchid Family

290. Showy Lady-slipper (*C. reginae*). Also called Pink-and-White Lady-slipper. Large lady-slipper with leafy stems, 2 to 3 feet tall. They end in 1 or 2 showy flowers. The rounded, inflated lip is 1 to 1½ inches long and is white, marked with pink or purple. Hairs on the leaves and stem sometimes cause a skin rash. Occurrence: Minnesota— swamps and moist woods in the north and east on limy, neutral soils; general—eastern U.S. and adjacent Canada.

Showy Lady-slipper is Minnesota's state flower. The plants are long-lived and slow to develop, requiring about 15 years from seed germination to flowering.

Orchid Family

291. Yellow Lady-slipper (*C. calceolus*). Leafy-stemmed lady-slipper, up to 2 feet tall, with flowers having an inflated, yellow lip. There are 2 American varieties: the **Large Yellow** (var. *pubescens*) has a lip or "slipper," usually 1¼ to 2 inches long, and purple-brown sepals; the **Small Yellow** (var. *parviflorum*) has a shorter lip and brownish-yellow sepals. The former is most common in woods, especially hardwood forests, and the latter in swamps and along shores. Occurrence: Minnesota—occasional throughout, except in the southwest; general—much of U.S. and adjacent Canada. Also in Eurasia.

Orchid Family

291. Yellow Lady-slipper. Late spring; summer.

292. White Lady-slipper. Late spring; summer.

292. White Lady-slipper (*C. candidum*). Low lady-slipper, usually less

293. Showy Orchis. Late spring.

than 1 foot tall, with leafy stems. The flower has an inflated, white lip ½ to 1 inch long that is veined with purple within. Occurrence: Minnesota — limy soils of undisturbed, moist prairies and edges of swamps in the south and west, now rare; general — from South Dakota east to the Atlantic Coast.

The **Ram's-head Lady-slipper** (*C. arietinum*) also occurs in Minnesota but is very rare. The small flower has a white lip veined with red. It grows on acid soil.

Orchid Family

ORCHIS (*Orchis*)

293. Showy Orchis (*O. spectabilis*).

Low perennial of hardwood forests. Usually 6 to 8 inches tall. It has 2 rather thick basal leaves and several small, spurred flowers in an elongate cluster. The lip is white. Other petals, and the sepals, are pink or purplish and unite to form a hood. Occurrence: Minnesota — mostly in the southeastern third, including the Twin Cities area, but now rare; general — eastern temperate North America.

If a pin is inserted into the spur of the flower, tiny club-shaped pollen masses will adhere to it. Such pollen masses (pollinia) are transported on the mouth parts of insects to the pistils of other flowers.

221

Orchid Family

294. Round-leaved Orchis (*O. rotundifolia*). Low plant of moist woods and swamps. It has a single basal leaf and a leafless stalk, usually 4 to 6 inches tall, on which are several spurred flowers. The lip of the flower is white spotted with purple and the other conspicuous flower parts are white to pale purple. Occurrence: Minnesota—mostly in the north in mossy, wooded swamps, especially under white cedar and tamarack trees; general—a northern orchid ranging from Greenland, Hudson Bay, and the Yukon south to northern U.S. In the far north it grows on open tundra.

294. Round-leaved Orchis. Spring; summer.

295. Purple Fringed Orchid. Summer.

Orchid Family

REIN ORCHID (*Habenaria*)

295. Purple Fringed Orchid (*H. psychodes*). Perennial of damp, open places. The leafy stem is erect, usually 1 to 2 feet tall, and ends in a showy cluster of small, purple flowers. These are about ½ inch across. The lip of the flower is 3-lobed and cut into a fringe. Occurrence: Minnesota—grassy and brushy marshes, mostly in the north and east; general—temperate eastern North America.

Ten other species of rein orchids are known from Minnesota. All are plants of bogs, marshes, and damp woods, and all have elongate clusters of flowers, each with a spur—the rein. Flowers are greenish, white, or pale yellow. The lip and other flower parts are of the same color, and the lip may or may not be fringed.

Orchid Family

DRAGON'S MOUTH (*Arethusa*)

296. Dragon's Mouth (*A. bulbosa*). A conspicuous and beautiful bog orchid. The stem, usually 6 to 8 inches tall, has a single leaf and ends in an odd-shaped flower about 1¼ inches across. The lip is pale pink dotted with yellow and purple. The ascending petals and sepals are a deeper pink. Occurrence: Minnesota—rare, in bogs and grassy swamps, mostly in the northeast; general—temperate eastern North America.

Two other conspicuous, rosy orchids with flowers about the same size grow in Minnesota bogs. The **Snake Mouth** (*Pogonia ophioglossoides*) has a solitary flower much like that of Dragon's Mouth but with a fringed lip. **Grass Pink** (*Calopogon pulchellus*) has a cluster of several pink flowers with spreading petals and sepals. The lip is at the top of the flower, in this respect differing from most other orchids.

296. Dragon's Mouth. Early summer.

297. Nodding Ladies' Tresses. Late summer; autumn

Orchid Family

LADIES' TRESSES (*Spiranthes*)

297. Nodding Ladies' Tresses (*S. cernua*). A small but beautiful orchid of late summer and autumn. The erect stem, usually less than 1 foot tall, ends in a spike of small, white flowers spirally arranged in 3 rows. They are markedly sweet-scented. Occurrence: Minnesota—throughout in prairies, meadows, and open forests; general—temperate eastern North America.

The **Hooded Ladies' Tresses** (*S. romanzoffiana*) is similar but the side and top sepals are united to form a hood. **Slender Ladies' Tresses** (*S. gracilis*) is a slender-stemmed species of dry, sandy places. Its flowers are in a single spiral.

223

298. Calypso. Early spring.

Orchid Family

CALYPSO (*Calypso*)

298. Calypso (*C. bulbosa*). Among the rarest and most beautiful of northern orchids. In early spring the short, flowering stalk, usually 2 to 5 inches tall, rises from the base of a broad leaf that has survived the winter. The flower has a slipper-shaped lip that is white marked with yellow, purple, and brown. Behind it are 5 narrow, purple petals and sepals, often standing erect much like the feathers on an Indian bonnet. Occurrence: Minnesota — rare, in coniferous forests, woods and swamps of the north; general — circumpolar. In North America south to northern U.S. and in mountains to Arizona.

Calypso was the nymph whose

224

charms delayed Ulysses for seven years on his journey home from Troy.

Orchid Family

RATTLESNAKE PLANTAIN
(*Goodyera*)

299. Dwarf Rattlesnake Plantain (*G. repens*). Also called Lattice-leaf. Small orchid of dry, open woodlands. Usually 4 to 10 inches tall and often growing in patches. The spikes of small, white flowers rise from a rosette of basal leaves, the blades of which are marked with white in a lattice pattern. Occurrence: Minnesota—most common in northern and central parts; general—subarctic regions south to eastern temperate North America.

Orchid Family

CORAL ROOT (*Corallorhiza*)

300. Spotted Coral Root (*C. maculata*). A saprophytic orchid that lives in partnership with a soil fungus and has no chlorophyll. The pinkish-purple stems, mostly less than 1 foot tall, rise from a mass of corallike roots. Leaves are reduced to sheaths, and the small flowers are in an elongate cluster. Petals and lip are white, usually tinted and spotted with purple. Occurrence: Minnesota—moist woods in north and east; general—much of temperate North America.

The **Early Coral Root** (*C. trifida*) has yellowish stems and flowers. **Striped Coral Root** (*C. striata*) has reddish-purple stems and purplish flowers with striped petals. Both species grow in moist woods.

Other orchids also live in partnership with a fungus but do not carry this relationship as far as do the coral roots.

299. Dwarf Rattlesnake Plantain. Summer.

300. Spotted Coral Root. Late spring; summer.

225

Index

Index

(Pages on which photographs of the flowers appear are italicized.)

234

236

The late **John Moyle,** who wrote the text of
Northland Wild Flowers, was a research
biologist and research supervisor in the
Minnesota Department of Natural Resources,
and a frequent contributor to *Minnesota
Volunteer.* **Evelyn Moyle** took most of the
photographs in this book. A former biology
instructor at the University of Minnesota, she
also lectures on wild flowers.